A Psychoanalyst's Quest

Other Books by Richard Robertiello

Voyage from Lesbos
A Handbook of Emotional Illness and Treatment
The Analyst's Role
Sexual Fulfillment and Self-Affirmation
Hold Them Very Close; Then Let Them Go
Your Own True Love
Big You—Little You
A Man in the Making

A Psychoanalyst's Quest

Richard C. Robertiello, M.D.

ST. MARTIN'S/MAREK
New York

Library of Congress Cataloging-in-Publication Data

Robertiello, Richard C.
    A psychoanalyst's quest.

    1. Robertiello, Richard C.   2. Psychoanalysts—United
States—Biography.   3. Psychotherapy.   I. Title.
RC339.52.R59A37   1986   616.89'17'0924 [B]   85-26113
ISBN 0-312-65239-9

First Edition

10 9 8 7 6 5 4 3 2 1

To Lucy

Contents

Acknowledgments

I wish to thank my editor, Joyce Engelson, and my agent, Don Congdon, for their invaluable help. I also want to thank my colleagues, Dr. Lawrence Hauser, Mr. Joseph Rizzo, Miss Lucy Smith, and Dr. Julius Weissman for their suggestions and contributions.

Foreword

Freud came to America in 1911, but it took about forty years for his concepts to become part, though often a banal part, of the general consciousness. Americans first became aware of psychoanalysis in the late 1940s, in part from reports of experiences of soldiers in World War II. Many of the soldiers who had been euphemistically designated as "gassed" in World War I were now more correctly seen by the general public to be psychiatric casualties. They may have been called victims of "battle fatigue," but they had been brought out of the closet as psychiatric rather than medical patients. Sodium Amytal, or Pentothal, or "truth serum" injections to "cure" battle dreams became household words. But it was really the movie *Spellbound* that brought psychoanalysis to broad popular consciousness. The theramin, a mysterious-sounding electronic instrument that was used to accompany the action in the movie, became the musical trademark in the media for the mysteries of the mind. There was a plethora of movies, radio shows, books, and—shortly thereafter—television shows that explored a now mysterious region: the mind. *The Snake Pit* with Olivia de Havilland was a movie about the horrors of a state mental hospital. Lucy Freeman's *Fight Against Fear* was a best-selling book about her own experiences as a patient in psychoanalysis. The denouement of Orson Welles's movie, *Citizen Kane,* involved the lifting of repression of the memory of the sled, Rosebud, that the central character had owned as a boy. Arthur Laurent's play, *A Clearing in the Woods,* was an exposition in dramatic form of a woman's unconscious. Even *Oklahoma* leaned on psychoanalysis in exposing the character of the villain, poor Jud.

In the late 1930s and early 1940s in high school and college, I had been fascinated by the ideas of psychoanalysis and had read whatever Freud I could get my hands on. But the thought of becoming a psychoanalyst seemed to me as remote a dream as pitching a no-hitter in the World Series for my favorite team, the New York Giants. Psychoanalysts, I thought, had an intelligence and a depth far beyond anything I could ever attribute to myself. But still I had been first in my class in high school, had gone to Harvard, and was in 1946 graduating from medical school at Columbia. I had taken my fourth-year elective in psychiatry at the mecca, New York State Psychiatric Institute, which many famous analysts attended.

I began hesitatingly to hope that my dream could come true. Could I possibly become one of these mysterious superhumans who were called psychoanalysts? Perhaps they were not born from the head of Zeus, but had in fact gone through the same educational process as I had done. Now that I had my M.D., I had acquired the key necessary at that time to enter this kingdom. Every time I went into the lobby of the Psychiatric Institute or onto one of the wards, I could hear the theramin play. I have had mystical peak experiences since then, viewing Michelangelo's *David* and the Taj Mahal. But each time I entered that building, I began a journey into the mysteries of the mind. I was "spellbound"—and the theramin played for me. This was even more exciting than pitching for the Giants. I wasn't only a hero, I was an explorer; but it was better than being Columbus or Vasco da Gama. My experience was really a 1946 version of *Close Encounters of the Third Kind*. It was spooky, magical, and eerie, more so even than man's first trip to the moon much later.

So I began to plan a path by which my fantasy and my reality might converge. My view then of psychoanalysts was that they were old, very wise, and had Viennese accents. But surely there had to be some young men to replace them. And if I thought clearly about it, who was better qualified than I to be one of them? On paper, anyway. Even if I did not have the wisdom or the accent, at least now I had the key. Perhaps I would try to use it. The worst they could do was exclude me, laugh at me when they saw how shallow and immature I was.

I ventured and somehow I was admitted into the fraternity. And I really got in on the ground floor. When I entered the field, America was practically virgin territory for psychoanalysis. I was fortunate to be there almost from the beginning. Yes, there had been a few American analysts before that time—mostly European refugees—but they had not yet begun seriously to impress the American public or even American medicine. Despite the small number of analysts, however, there had already been some splits in the psychoanalytic community; psychoanalysts have never been able to get along. How can there be two or more omniscient gods in one analytic society? They had fought before and since then have continued to fight among themselves, ostensibly about their theoretical and clinical differences, but often actually about their omnipotence and grandiosity.

Fortunately, at least from the viewpoint of gaining a historical perspective, I have been on the scene during these later developments in American psychoanalysis. And also perhaps fortunately, I was never able to maintain the rigid, unyielding point of view that some of my colleagues have managed to adhere to for almost forty years. For many of them, time has passed but nothing has really changed since Freud died in 1939. Freud, as we shall see, focused his attention on instincts, drive theory, and the Oedipus complex. On the other hand, I, starting my studies with Freudian concepts, have been drawn to many varied analytic theories. Perhaps that is my strength as well as my weakness. I have been drawn sometimes briefly, sometimes more consistently to the works of Adolph Meyer, Clara Thompson, Karen Horney, Sandor Rado, John Rosen, the Zen-Buddhist analysts, Timothy Leary, Donald W. Winnicott, Harry Guntrip, Margaret Mahler, Heinz Kohut, Carl Jung, and lately Melanie Klein. In this book I will try to examine the impact of the changes in social climate in America on my personal psychological changes, and on the changes in my attachments to different psychoanalytic theories and techniques.

One thing that has never changed in me since adolescence is my mystical sense of wonder, my thrill at the search into mysterious regions. Each new analytic development has ushered in a new set of mysteries to be explored. I think that life without passion is a living death. My particular passion has always been and continues to be this search into the mysterious, obscure, mystical unknown. Perhaps after forty years it seems naive but it's still a great metaphor—I can still see Ingrid Bergman analyzing Gregory Peck in *Spellbound,* discovering that the reason for his amnesia was his guilt over his brother's death. And I can hear the theramin playing its eerie music in the background.

Introduction

I think it is important to distinguish between theory and "technique" in psychoanalysis. Even though I have broken almost every possible rule of technique that has been laid down by the followers of Freud in America, I am a strong believer in theory. My first two supervisors in psychoanalysis gave me a very solid theoretical base. They taught me the science of psychoanalysis: that what happens in one session is predictable from the previous one; that dreams involve a sequential unfolding of the unconscious; that a session has a central theme that makes it cohesive. One of the strongest, most admirable aspects of classical psychoanalysis is its insistent emphasis on the science of psychoanalysis. Classical analysts—perhaps to a fault—try to integrate their theories and techniques out of a body of knowledge that stays consistent in its point of view. Classical analysts attempt to minimize the role of personality of the analyst in order to maintain an objective stance in which a certain amount of statistical and objective validation can be applied.

I will always applaud these attempts to instill scientific thinking in psychoanalysis. For this reason I am in disagreement with so-called California-type analysts and many humanistic or existential analysts. (Obviously, I am not disparaging all analysts in California. One of the best analysts in this country, in my opinion, is James Grotstein in Los Angeles.) These analysts, in general, say that rather than the application of a scientific theory, it is only the analyst's being real and authentic that makes people better. Of course, I believe that an analyst should be human and authentic; I place a high premium on creating that kind of environment in the office. I am also a strong believer in the idea that a great deal that goes on and is creative in psychoanalysis has nothing to do with its so-called scientific aspects, but rather with the patient's internalizing aspects of the analyst that he admires, such as his authenticity, caring, dedication, and integrity. However, one can get these responses from a relative or friend. The analyst needs to have, in addition to these personal qualities, a vast body of knowledge that is stored in his "computer," available to help him understand and explain to the patient just exactly what is going on in his unconscious as well as his conscious mind.

There has been an increasing emphasis during the past few years on the importance of cognitive processes, that is, the patient's intellectual insight, in psychoanalysis. Some of Freud's early papers emphasized that the "cure" came from the release of suppressed emotion by the patient. The patient, and perhaps even the analyst, did not really have to understand what was happening as long as some cathartic release was achieved. I am a very strong supporter of the idea that—at least for relatively stable neurotic patients—it is essential for both analyst and patient to have a very clear concept of exactly what is unfolding in the analytic process and how it connects with the material of previous sessions. Emotional release or behavioral change may follow, but cognition is often the means of opening the door. I will never accept the statement from a supervisee that the patient is getting better, but he has no idea why this is happening. So conducting analysis without a strong theoretical base makes absolutely no sense to me. It is analogous to performing surgery with a dull spoon.

On the other hand, one of the big problems in psychoanalysis has been that many of its most brilliant theoreticians have been quite lacking in interpersonal skills. Often they have been very uncomfortable in looking at people while trying to communicate their excellent understanding to their patients. They might have been brilliant at figuring out what was going on, but they were unable to be warm, caring, communicative, and emotionally interactive. Freud is the best example of such a person. He admitted very explicitly that he felt uneasy about facing his patients or interacting with them in a warm, emotional, human manner. He was very pleased at being able to sit behind a supine patient on the couch. His personal neurosis led him and his followers in the American Psychoanalytic Association to adopt this totally stilted and artificial position between analyst and patient, and this has had very serious effects on the analytic process. Many people, including myself, feel that this artificial *un*human (not inhuman) setting for an interpersonal encounter creates many of the problems that it then sets about to "cure."

I remember when I myself was first a patient on the couch, the setting evoked a tremendous idealization of the analyst and minimized me. Granted, this may have been part of my own problem. I may have been searching for a father I could idealize and subsequently internalize. There had been major defects in my father's relationship to me. Still, this problem was mitigated when I insisted on a face-to-face encounter with my analyst. I also remember vividly when I started practicing analysis and sometimes sat behind the couch. First of all, this procedure increased my confidence and diminished my interpersonal anxiety considerably. I did not have to be looked at and the distance made me feel superior and safer. Secondly, it was much easier than doing analysis the way I do it now. I could relax because I was not being scrutinized. I could even drift off into reveries and fantasies of my own. I was not intimately involved with another person, even if I was with his verbal productions.

Actually, the very word "technique," when it is used to describe the method of applying theory, repels me. It is not a "technique" that one uses in the sense of its being a learned programmed response. Rather, the way to be in the room with the patient is to *be there,* to be communicative, to be involved. The analyst must allow his own feelings, fantasies, and unconscious to lead him. But—and it is a very important but—he does not behave exactly the same way he might in some other intimate relationship. He must filter his emotions through his cognition, so that he can understand the meaning of the encounter as well as experiencing it. Harry Stack Sullivan, the American psychoanalyst, was certainly on the right track when he spoke of the analyst's being a "participant observer."

There was an enormously brilliant analyst, a follower of Melanie Klein, named Heinrich Racker, who alas did not achieve much fame. This was due partly to his working in Argentina and being a follower of Melanie Klein rather than Freud, and partly to his untimely death in 1958. Racker's idea was that anything that goes on in the room between patient and analyst is emotionally charged and should be the main content of what should be explored. He advocated the analyst's paying exquisite attention to his own feelings and using them as a guide to what the patient was expressing. For instance, if I as an analyst have sexual feelings, I should not dismiss them as coming out of my own frustrations, but should wonder what this particular patient is doing to stimulate these feelings. After all, I may not have had these feelings about any other patient that day. And though the patient's verbal communications may deal with her problems with her job or her children, the main total communication (including nonverbal) may be seductive. This could be conveyed through body language and tone of voice rather than words. Obviously, one can carry this too far. Still, all that can be analyzed appropriately is what is going on in the room. And in truth the same issues might very well not be raised if the patient were in the room with a different analyst. Who the analyst is *as a real person* has a great deal to do with what the patient's responses are. Thus, the orthodox Freudian premise that the analyst is a blank screen, a tabula rasa, onto which the patient projects his or her unconscious, is, I now believe, a false one. Hiding behind the couch does not negate the impact of his personality. However, it does help an uncomfortable analyst to avoid dealing with his own feelings and the impact of his idiosyncratic personality on the patient and on the analytic process.

In this book, I shall attempt to reconstruct the very circuitous path that brought me to my current analytic views. As I set out, I will be trying, too, to answer questions about myself and about my evolution as an analyst in terms of both the ongoing changes in myself and in analytic theory. In what ways have I changed emotionally since I became an analyst? Why has the Freudian body of early analytic thought become overlayed with later theorizations for me? How did my clinical experience and my personal life experience influence changes in my work as an analyst? What was the impact of changes in the world around me, both the macrocosm and the microcosm, on my way of practicing psychoanalysis?

I have been and continue to be involved in a quest for knowledge about myself, my patients, and the world around me. Being a psychoanalyst gives me the opportunity to pursue this quest most of my waking hours.

1
The Beginning

In writing about the evolution of my thinking as an analyst, I must first write about who I am, where I came from, what kind of a person I was, and what kind I have become. The fact that specific theories of psychoanalysis have had such an impact on me is not a function of my having a special pipeline to the Truth. Instead, it is the result of a very subjective group of choices that fit in with my character, and, even more, with my character at a particular period of my life. At some periods I have been one of the most uptight, compulsive conformists and at others one of the most iconoclastic rebels, not only in my analytic thinking but in my behavior, my lifestyle, and my transcendent interests. I think it behooves me, especially since I am an analyst, to attempt to understand the meaning of my choices of theory and technique not only as a function of my intellect but also of my character.

With this in mind, I shall proceed to violate one of the basic tenets of classical psychoanalysis—the taboo against self-revelation by the analyst. Classical analysts of course feel that any personal knowledge the patient has about the analyst contaminates the patient's responses and "dilutes" or tampers with reactions that the patient would have to a "blank screen." I shall discuss the pros and cons of this position in a subsequent chapter. At this time what I can say is that I have no objection whatsoever to my patients—past, present, and future—having this knowledge about me. In fact, I have written another book, *A Man in the Making,* which is much more self-revealing than this one. I believe that psychoanalysis is an interactive process within a relationship, rather than an individual self-revelation in the presence of an observer; therefore, who the analyst really is as a person has an enormous impact on the patient's words and feelings. So the patient's knowing who the analyst is can help clarify the nature of this particular patient's reactions to this particular analyst. I shall elaborate on this theme later.

First of all, I am different from almost every other analyst because I come from an Italo-American background. I was at a party a few years ago at which I was one of four such analysts. One of them said that if a bomb were dropped on the building, Italo-American analysts would be wiped out in one fell swoop. An exaggeration, of course. However, an extremely low percentage of analysts, especially in New York City, are Italian. Until very recently it was considered bad taste, if not outright prejudice, to suggest that one's ethnic background had an impact of rather large proportions on character development. Now we have an opposite trend. Some patients of mine are engaged in what is termed "ethnotherapy." Just recently when I enquired as to the meaning of this word, I was told it consisted of getting together a group of people with similar ethnic backgrounds to share their experiences—both positive and negative—about their ethnicity.

My father and both of my grandfathers were very strong, autocratic patriarchal figures. My mother and both grandmothers were extremely weak, docile, servile, submissive women. I am not implying that this is always the case in Italo-American homes, but it often tends to be. In my family there was an extreme of this pattern. My paternal grandmother, who lived in the same house with us until I was fifteen, could not read or write and did not speak any English; in fact, to my recollection she never ever went outside the house. She had no say in any discussion—not even in what food was bought for her to cook. She was referred to as "the Saint"; in actuality, she was more a slave and a nonentity. My maternal grandmother was somewhat less subservient since she had been born and educated in America and spoke English well. Still, my maternal grandfather, who was a doctor in New York for over fifty years, maintained a style of life that varied very little from that of his counterpart in a small town in southern Italy. Despite being a doctor, he spoke very little English and that very badly. Like many other Italian men, he was waited on hand and foot by the women in the house. He insisted on perfect silence during his meals, had his wine and mineral water, his daily siesta, and total freedom to leave his wife and children for months at a time to return to his hometown in Italy, where he pursued his interest in hunting—not only animals, but other women.

So, a very strong patriarchal structure was part of my background and certainly of my southern Italian heritage. I think this heritage and my most important male role models had an influence on my becoming a person who tended to follow his idiosyncratic inclinations rather than another person's doctrinaire views. Being my own man and "doing it my way" were traits that were rewarded by my family and were exemplified by my male role models. My maternal grandfather was an outstanding example of a man who followed his own star and refused to become Americanized even after fifty years in this country. Similarly, I could never accept following one school of psychoanalytic thought, but was always seeking a way that fit in best with my own personality. Also, since my paternal grandfather needed me to be outstanding, as I shall shortly describe, I could never accept being one of a group of followers; I was programmed by him to be a leader from the start.

But growing up male and Italo-American in the 1920s, thirties, and forties meant more than just coming from that kind of family structure and developing a sense of machismo. It meant being part of a severely denigrated minority. Even though my maternal grandfather, my father, and two of my uncles by marriage were doctors, there were very few Italian-Americans who had made a special mark in *any* public arena in those days. My family and extended family felt it to be a disgrace and a humiliation to be Italo-American; they did not have the pride in their ethnicity that Jews or Irish-Americans seemed to have. I was brought up to feel that being Italian meant being on the bottom of the totem pole, only above what were then called Negroes. My aunt, Filomena, changed her name to Dolores and pretended to be Spanish. (That was obviously before the Puerto Rican influx into New York and the rise in prejudices against Hispanics.) My father, a prominent doctor, felt honored if a Jew or Irish-American came to dinner. He did not even aspire to having a WASP friend—an unattainable goal. Not until I was thirty years old and went to Italy did I begin to have a feeling of pride about my heritage. This circumstance no doubt contributed to my mistrusting the establishment and my having a tendency to rebel against it. I started out with the feeling that I would never be accepted anyway because of my ethnicity, so I had little to lose by not trying to fit in.

But there were even more unusual influences at work than my ethnic background. My mother was a particularly passive and anxious person. Very early in my childhood, certainly before the age of three, she turned me over to my paternal grandfather. He was looking for someone to redeem his frustrated life, and he was delighted to have me as the object for this. So basically I was a male child brought up by a man. After age two, I slept every night until the age of twelve in the same room as my paternal grandfather and grandmother. But beyond this my grandfather was charged with my toilet training, my homework supervision, my discipline—as applied by his belt—and my overall parenting. My mother and father both completely abdicated their roles to him: my father because he was so busy being a doctor, and my mother because she was so anxious and immature.

My grandfather was an incredibly harsh disciplinarian. He *really* believed in "all work and no play." He had me in such rigorous training that I was able to tell time at three and read at four. My grandfather had wanted to become a professional, but since there was only enough money to send one son to college in Naples, his brother was given the privilege. According to family legend, this brother squandered his time and money on wine and women and my grandfather was forced to become a tailor. Since I was chosen to be my grandfather's narcissistic extension and to live out the life he had been unable to realize, he wanted to be very sure I would not travel the same path as his older brother.

So well did he indoctrinate me that when at five I was sent to kindergarten, I refused to stay there. Why should I waste my time playing all day, when there was work to be done! Five-year-old Richard must have stunned the kindergarten teacher. She called the principal into the situation. Finally, not knowing what else to do, the school put me in the first grade. By five Grandpa had already trained me to renounce all pleasure for work; in fact, he would scream at me if he caught me listening to "Jack Armstrong, the All-American Boy" for fifteen minutes on the radio. An interesting postscript to my adventure as a five-year-old is that I refused to stay in the first grade unless my mother was there with me. The school allowed her to stay for almost two weeks, but this time the principal intervened and insisted on her leaving. This was accompanied by immense furor on my part and a giant temper tantrum. The principal, however, unlike my mother, did not yield, and I was finally launched alone into my school career.

I believe my ability to manipulate my mother has made me very sensitive to patients who attempt to manipulate me or others—"It takes one to know one." This, in turn, has led me to have a great interest in those psychoanalytic theorists who focus their attention on the analysis of character and of styles of life and interpersonal maneuvers, such as manipulation, rather than on the exposition of the unconscious alone. Classical analysts tend to be silent and nonintervening, and to allow their patients an orderly unfolding of their unconscious. Some other analysts—starting with

Wilhelm Reich, followed by Alfred Adler, Karen Horney, and Edward Bergler, among others—focused their attention on the analyst's intruding and "attacking" the style in which a patient leads his or her life and deals with people. They postulated that the patient's character—obsessive-compulsive, paranoid, passive-dependent, and so on—was a way of containing and masking his basic unconscious conflicts. They felt that unless the patient's character and way of being in the world was punctured and softened by the analyst's active intervention, the exposure of his unconscious would have little effect on his psyche.

My initial skip of a grade was followed by several others, so that I graduated from grammar school at twelve, from high school at fifteen, from college at nineteen, and medical school at age twenty-two. My grandfather had done his job well. I followed his program, becoming a dedicated, compulsive worker and a professional. Still today if I make a mistake or spend too much time or money on myself, I get anxious that I may get a strapping from my internalized grandfather's belt. Also, in retrospect, what a strong-willed little boy—like my male role models—to be able not only to get my way about going into the first grade but also about having my mother there. One must remember this was long before there was any hint of permissive education in public schools.

In the elementary and high schools I attended, I was exposed to the three R's and strict discipline. A strong will, as well as a compulsive need for work and self-denial, have been important parts of my personality. But along with these has existed a feeling of panic about being alone without a surrogate. My need to be perfect in order to avoid my grandfather's punishment has made me a prodigious worker. It has also made me dissatisfied with any level of proficiency I may have accomplished. Ninety-nine percent out of a hundred was totally unsatisfactory for my grandfather. Having incorporated him into my internal world, 99 percent has been unsatisfactory for me as well. I have always gone on reading, attending lectures, teaching, discussing issues with my colleagues in an attempt to continue to change and grow. Even now, after thirty-five years of practice, I spend some Sunday evenings in an informal seminar with colleagues discussing the meaning of therapy as it fits into a person's view of life. This insistence on constant growth reflects, at least in part, my continuing, futile attempts to avoid my grandfather's punishment and my mother's abandonment. I never achieved either of these goals in my real life. Furthermore, my search for different ideas could be likened to my attempt to find a mother who would provide a structure for me in which I might feel secure against abandonment—another goal I have never completely achieved either in my professional or personal life. So I have tended, especially early in my career, to react to each patient as if he/she were a punitive grandfather and a potentially abandoning mother. This made me maximize my efforts to do a good job to avoid either punishment or abandonment by my patients.

There was one other crucial theme in my early childhood that has had a very important impact on my psyche. I have described a really bleak household. My mother was weak, passive, and easily manipulated. My grandmother, "the Saint," was so much of a perfect zero that I cannot even recall having a sense of loss after her death. My paternal grandfather was totally lacking in any affection or compassion for me, and interested only in my achievement. My father was interested only in his own growing professional success—he too had been subjected to my grandfather—and, like many Italian men, wanted to be the sole recipient of my mother's affection. He saw me as a hated rival who had displaced him in his own father's attention and was a threat to displace him in his wife's. His competitiveness with me stirred up an equal amount of competitiveness in me, toward him. My survival, as I perceived it, depended on my being able to defeat him. One of the main arenas for our struggle was to become the medical profession: Who would be the better doctor? Since my sense of survival depended on my victory over him, I had to become a better doctor than he. The areas he valued were knowledge, competence, conscientiousness, and availability to patients. My need to overcome him contributed to the energy I devoted to these areas.

The only bright spot in this dismal picture was my sister, who was two years younger than I. She was beautiful, sweet, adoring of me, my sole ally and occasional playmate. I was jealous of her charisma and of the fact that she had completely displaced me in everyone's affection, but I also loved her tremendously and felt a strong bond to her. She was the only light of my life. When I was seven and she was five, she died of a mastoid infection. No one in the family seemed to be concerned about my feelings (I was not even allowed to attend her funeral). I do not remember going through a process of grieving. I think I must have dealt with my pain by shutting off my feelings and subsequently being very wary about surrendering my love to another person for fear that I would again be abandoned and be subjected to the same painful loss. I do think this devastating loss in childhood has made me especially sensitive to the pain my patients suffer. Their pain in one sense becomes my pain. I have a tremendous motivation to help put an end to it: it is very difficult for me to turn my back on a person in pain. This has undoubtedly also influenced my eschewing the cold, objective, nongratifying stance taken by many psychoanalysts. In contrast, I make it a point to let my patients know that I am constantly available to them for a comforting twenty-four hours a day. I cannot tolerate from my own experience a person in emotional pain, especially over a loss, who has no one in his environment to comfort him.

Religion was not a very big issue in our home. We were nominally Roman Catholic, but no one took this very seriously except for me. My father and grandfather were atheists; my grandmother "did not exist." My mother went to church fairly regularly on Sundays, but more because she was obedient than out of any conviction. I was looking for some kind of salvation from my bleak existence. So from age seven on, when I received my first communion, I turned to Catholicism for some kind of spirituality and faith, as there was no one and nothing in my home I could turn to for comfort or hope. But gradually this faith was eroded. After I had witnessed nuns hitting children over the head with rulers and seen priests utterly lacking in spirituality, I was ripe to turn to another faith when I entered high school at twelve.

The school I was sent to was the honor high school for New York City, Townsend Harris, and one could enter only through competitive examinations. Since the Jewish culture valued educational excellence, the enrollment was 99 percent Jewish. I was practically the only Italian-American in the school, despite the fact that the Italo-American population at the time in 1936 was the largest ethnic group in New York City. In Townsend Harris, they used to say that the Christian Club meetings were held in the telephone booth. So here I was at age twelve, disillusioned with my Catholicism, a very compulsive student, practically the youngest in the class, thrown in with a group of Jews.

It seemed to me that most of these bright Jewish boys were atheists, communists, or socialists, very interested in psychological ideas and in Freud in particular. The Civil War was going on in Spain and the students were active in raising money to defeat Franco. Coming out of the Great Depression, socialism as represented by Norman Thomas still seemed a possibility for our government, although Franklin D. Roosevelt had preempted many of the American liberals. There was obviously a faulty distribution of the wealth. My millionaire aunt and uncle had three maids, a cook and a chauffeur, and a summer and winter palace, while people stood on bread lines and sold apples. Secretaries made fifteen or twenty dollars a week. Capitalism did not seem like the best system for most of the people.

I worked very hard—hard enough to be number one in

my class and to get into Harvard. I relinquished the rem-
nants of my faith rapidly, under the influence of my peers.
Since I was more spiritual in my quest than political, I was
never seriously taken with socialism or communism as were
some of my classmates. However, my new religion became
psychology—and especially Freudian psychoanalysis. It of-
fered some new hope for relieving my pain and making my
enormous anxiety bearable. I talked about it at length with
my schoolmates and read some of Freud. At last I had found
a way of trying to understand the reasons for such tremendous anxiety and insecurity. Of course, I was very competitive scholastically. During my three years at Townsend
Harris I literally "burned the midnight oil." I was a prodigious reader in addition to studying for my courses. I had
to be the best; that was the only position my grandfather—
then external and now taken into my internal world—
would accept. I was in a constant panic in school for fear of
not maintaining my position. And my competition were the
brightest boys in New York City, so my goal was not easily
attained or maintained. Grandpa insisted on my being first
in my class and I had internalized this into my self-esteem
system. If I could not be the most perfect hero, I was a total
zero.

After being "led away" from my Catholic faith in high
school, I was exposed to ever more "corrupting" influences
at Harvard. Here again, in the class of 1943, I found myself
to be just about the youngest in my class and one of four
Italian-Americans in a class of a thousand. At Harvard in the
early 1940s, the WASPs did not talk to anyone who was not
a WASP. So, my friends were again almost exclusively Jewish, except for one of the four or five blacks in my class.
Again I was exposed to more atheism, very liberal politics,
and to Sigmund Freud. In fact, six out of my group of ten
or so very close friends ended up as psychoanalysts. In college there were endless bull sessions about the meaning of
life; Freud and psychoanalysis played an important role in
our thinking. Also I discovered quickly that, though I could

do very well academically at Harvard (I made the Dean's List and was awarded an honorary scholarship during my first year), there was no way to satisfy Grandpa's requirement to be number one academically. At Harvard the competition was just too strong.

My unconscious, with some cooperation from my hormonal system, came up with a new field of competition. I would try to become the most successful lover in my class, or at least within my subgroup. This compromise both acceded to my grandfather's request to be number one and rebelled against his wishes by following the path of his hated libertine older brother. After my first year I rarely if ever made Dean's List. Instead I had to excel as a lover. Any failure was met with the same unrelenting self-flagellation. I was not allowed to live in peace by my internalized grandfather if I had any failures. So, whenever I was either actually rejected or felt that I had been, I fell into intense periods of self-hatred and depression and began very seriously to contemplate suicide. This situation also replayed my mother's abandonment. My uncle—my mother's younger brother and one of my male role models in my early childhood—had killed himself over a love affair when he was nineteen and I was five. Secretly, I thought I would follow in his footsteps.

In any event, as a result of my anxiety, depression, and suicidal preoccupation, as well as my interest in psychiatry, I had my first contact with psychiatry at sixteen when I reported to the Student Health at Harvard and asked to see a psychiatrist. I was madly in love with a girl but felt—probably correctly at the time—that she did not return my affection in kind. The doctor I saw was very likely a general practitioner who fancied himself a psychiatrist. I told him about my terrible emotional pain, heightened by feelings of physical ugliness because of adolescent acne. As I recall, he was a pleasant, open, warm fellow, an Italian-American like me. He told me I should not worry because I was an attractive young man and he was sure I would do well with girls.

I suppose I felt somewhat better for the reassurance. Even at age sixteen, though, I think I wondered whether this was all there was to psychiatry. It certainly was not what I had read in Freud.

Indeed, in 1940 in America most of the psychiatrists were "alienists," doctors working in state mental hospitals whose function was to diagnose insane people and then supervise what was tantamount to their incarceration. I say supervise, because there was no real treatment for them. Even for most neurotic patients there was little treatment available other than from the handful of psychoanalysts. In fact, the psychiatrist who saw me was quite remiss. I was terribly anxious and depressed and a real suicide risk. A little later, with the very conscious idea of following in my uncle's footsteps and feeling rejected by a woman, I made a serious suicide attempt that was aborted by very fortuitous and un-expected circumstances. But even after this attempt, the Student Health made no effort to follow up on my situation or offer me any psychiatric help. So my personal experi-ences with psychiatry during my college years were not very encouraging.

The discussions that took place with my peers about the nature of the unconscious were more illuminating than any contact I had with the profession. Aside from the handful of European psychoanalysts who had come to America and settled mainly in New York, there were very few American psychiatrists who had much expertise in treating people with neurotic problems in the early 1940s. The fact that the Student Health at Harvard, the mecca of learning, was so remiss in my case was a rather typical example of the gen-eral state of the profession in America at that time.

2
Medical School

In 1941 the war began. I was graduated from Harvard in 1943, and came back to New York City and to Columbia. Many of my classmates at Harvard died in action. I was accepted by Columbia Medical School and so deferred from military service. But three months after starting, all of us medical students were put into the Army; too many of us would have left school and volunteered unless we were in uniform. The feeling about World War II was very different from that of either the Korean or the Vietnam wars. Now that the Army was paying my way through medical school and giving me a subsistence allowance, I was able to get married at age twenty. Ironically, the woman I married was the same one I had felt was jilting me the year before, which had led to my suicide attempt. The jilting had existed only in my mind, undoubtedly a replay of my experience with my mother. "The greatest tragedies in my life are the ones that never happened."

In medical school, I dreamed of being launched on my journey toward the goal of becoming a psychoanalyst, still a very remote dream for me and one I scarcely hoped to achieve. I was not encouraged by the medical school training I received in psychiatry. I am sure my memory is not too much at fault; as I recall, we had no specific course in psychiatry at all. Instead, we had a series of lectures, not more than ten in all, throughout our four years of medical school. These were lectures by a nondescript group of physicians, some of whom resembled or were in fact the alienists in state hospitals. They dealt almost exclusively with diagnoses of the major psychoses—schizophrenia and

13

manic-depressive psychosis—and very little with the neuroses. There was hardly a mention of psychoanalysis. My father used to call psychiatrists "the garbagemen of medicine"; in fact in those days in the early forties this was mostly true. Doctors who were too inept to practice medicine or surgery drifted into psychiatry. They were mostly connected with state hospitals, lived in remote parts of the states, with quarters in the hospitals. It was rumored that one couldn't tell the doctors from the patients without a scorecard. One thing that was mentioned in the lectures in medical school was two new forms of treatment for the major psychoses. The first was electric shock therapy, which had been introduced into the United States by an Italian, Renato Almansi. The second was insulin shock therapy.

During my stay in medical school, the war ended. In 1945 there was a climate of hope for building a better world. America was deluged by stories of the enormous numbers of psychiatric casualties and some of the miraculous psychiatric cures with Sodium Amytal, the "truth serum." The typical case report was of the soldier whose best buddy had been shot beside him. The patient developed anxiety and had recurrent battle dreams, reliving the battlefield experience frequently and waking up in a cold sweat. The psychiatrist would inject Sodium Amytal intravenously and make the patient relive the scene. He would also lightly explore any psychological reactions the patient might have had to the experience: guilt, remorse, grief. Often this process cured the patient of his anxiety and his recurrent nightmares.

This treatment got the medical profession and the general public interested in psychiatry as a *psychological* method of cure, not just of diagnosis or the administering of shock treatment. As a result, instead of the people at the bottom of the class in medical school choosing psychiatry, some of the brightest, most intellectual ones began to do so. Psychiatry gradually became more closely associated with psychoanalysis and the exploration of the psyche, whereas before it had been associated—correctly so—with custodial care, and more recently with the application of shock therapy. These treatments hardly appealed to the intellect. Meanwhile the media began to be filled with stories with a psychoanalytic base.

In 1946—the year of *Spellbound*—I was graduated from medical school. During the last quarter of my final year I had had the opportunity of choosing an elective, and I chose psychiatry. Simultaneously I had begun to experience an exacerbation of overwhelming anxiety and depression, perhaps because now I would really have to test my mettle as a doctor, and my father had convinced me that I would be totally inept. Not having learned from my experience at Harvard, I went once again to the Student Health. There I was seen for a few brief sessions by one of the most prominent men in American psychiatry. He was a clinical professor of psychiatry at Columbia, and taught in the Psychoanalytic School at Columbia. He was a sort of American version of Colonel Blimp, stuffy and very proper, busy making money in his private practice. So he turned me over to a less illustrious colleague of his who was destined to achieve a certain degree of fame as a psychoanalyst. I was twenty-two at this time; she must have been at least in her middle forties. I do not think even she would find it indelicate for me to say she was not one of the world's foremost beauties. Nevertheless, I fell very much in love with her. I kept trying to see if she wore a wedding ring (though, of course, I was married). I had very romantic and sexual feelings about her. For the first time, I found out what an erotic transference was. When I began to see my own patients, I was to find out what an erotic countertransference was. Transferences are, of course, strong, insistent, inappropriate feelings the patient has toward the analyst, repetitions of previous feelings toward family members in childhood. Countertransference is the same kind of feeling on the part of the analyst for the patient. My analyst was a very nervous, thin, wiry, chain-smoking Bette Davis type. I do not know if I made her even more nervous by my overwhelming anxiety and depression and my erotic transference. In any event, either because of some countertransference *she* had or because I was a free patient through Student Health, she too made short shrift of me and dismissed me after seeing me once or twice a week, sitting up, for a couple of months. This dismissal was to prove rather ill-advised in the light of subsequent events. So I had been to two "for-real" psychoanalysts and had come away empty-handed. Counting my friend at the Harvard Student Health, that was three down and about another ten to go (so far!).

Although my experience as a patient had been rather unrewarding, my experience on the other side of the fence was much more gratifying. I started my elective quarter in psychiatry at the Psychiatric Institute and Vanderbilt Clinic in New York. To me this was almost a holy place. In fact, I experienced many of the same spiritual sensations on entering its hallowed halls and subsequently its locked wards that I had experienced in Catholic churches during the years from seven to twelve when I was a believer. I was assigned also to see some outpatients in Vanderbilt Clinic of Presbyterian Hospital. I remember how inadequate and terrified I felt at twenty-two to be advising fifty-year-olds on their marital and sexual problems. Luckily I looked old for my age. But, to be sure I would not appear too ludicrous, I grew a mustache. Thank God, I was dark and fairly hirsute.

In any event the patients did not mock me for my immaturity; they were too involved with their own troubles. But the high spot of my senior-year elective was being assigned a beautiful, bright, blond young lady my own age as an inpatient. Naturally, I fell madly in love with her. Countertransference is a fairly ubiquitous problem in fledgling therapists. I used to go into Mecca, up to the ward, open the door with my key, lock it, and then enter a plain cubicle with this lovely sweet Lorelei. I am sure that in my unconscious I was a little boy and she was my sister. I would sit and talk to her about the hospital, how she felt, her family.

Nothing extraordinary was happening except that I thought she was the most beautiful, sweet lovely lady I had ever met. She spoke perfectly normally. I could not even understand why she had been diagnosed as schizophrenic.

Then one day, presumably after I had gained her confidence, she told me about a "dream lover" she had. He would come down to make love to her and give her orgasms at least ten times a day. I was crestfallen. I realized I could be no match for her psychosis. Actually verbal psychotherapy, even by an experienced therapist, usually has little impact on the progression of a psychosis. Strangely enough, I ran into her at a state hospital two years later. Her beauty had completely faded—she looked burned out, washed out, and had the pasty skin and pallor of institutionalized psychotics. She also had that empty look in the eyes: I could look into her eyes without getting a reflective response from her. So much for *my* dream lover, my first real patient as a fledgling psychiatrist.

There was much more to my senior elective. The institute was one of the hubs of the psychoanalytic movement in America in the mid-1940s and many famous professionals taught there. I attended conferences and heard these people and others talking about the Oedipus complex and other aspects of Freud's work. Sandor Rado, who was one of the most megalomanic analysts ever (and that's saying a lot) gave a lecture on how he would have cured the patients Freud had failed to cure. Perhaps the most famous analyst there was John Rosen. He started a whole new form of treatment that he called Direct Analysis, about which he subsequently wrote a book. He would verbalize what he thought was going on in the patient's primitive unconscious. Actually, I am not sure whether he was exposing the patient's unconscious or his own conscious thinking accompanied by one of the foulest mouths in town. I was sitting in on his sessions in order to learn his technique. A very proper WASP lady would walk into the room staring into space. "You would like to take my big cock and put it in your mouth and suck on it," said Rosen. I nearly fell out of my chair.

The interview proceeded along these lines. People thought Rosen was a genius and a courageous man; I wondered whether he was a con artist. He subsequently wrote a paper stating that he had cured thirty out of thirty-one schizophrenics using this treatment. Every rich schizophrenic in the world came to see him. He acquired so much money that he started the Doylestown Foundation in Doylestown, Pennsylvania. Ten years later, a follow-up of his thirty-one patients showed that twenty-one of them were psychotic. The normal remission rate for untreated schizophrenia is 33 percent, the same as his "cure" rate.

Later on in my career I ran across another team of doctors who said they could cure schizophrenia with histamine. They too made millions. I was one of a team who tried to verify their results. The patients who received histamine had exactly the same rate of remission as those who received placebos. (The only valid kind of test in medicine is the double-blind test, in which neither the patient nor the doctor knows whether the patient is getting the drug or a placebo.) I was thus taught to be equally wary of people who say they can cure cancer with creamed spinach or vitamin E, without this kind of testing of their thesis.

In any event my fantasy of becoming an analyst received a big impetus from my senior elective. I saw some great names and realized they were all too human, so I knew I was not totally a fool rushing in where angels feared to tread. By the time I was graduated from medical school, I had begun to believe that I might be able to contribute to this new field, psychoanalysis. I had also developed a disdain for "normal" doctors (like my father), whom I considered mere technicians. Psychoanalysts, on the other hand, I saw as creative philosophers. I had found a way of defeating my father. Now however I had to live through my internship, which meant returning to a medical setting and struggling to become this "mere" technician.

3

Internship

Internship meant leaving psychiatry for fifteen months and rotating through different medical and surgical services in the city hospital I chose. I delivered seventy babies, sewed up wounds, set fractures, did minor operations, drew blood, did spinal taps, administered anesthesia, and treated hundreds of patients. This is quite a strain under normal circumstances, but my internship began in 1946. Many doctors were still in the Army, so the resident and attending staffs were reduced. Those doctors who were back from the Army were busy trying to reestablish their private practices. I and my fellow interns, who had hardly ever treated a patient and had never before had the responsibility for patient care, were suddenly thrust into a medical bedlam in an understaffed hospital. Often one student nurse was in charge of hundreds of patients. Operations were done by poorly trained surgeons. I literally had to carry bedpans and trays because the hospital was so understaffed.

In this dramatic situation, I was up every other night and every other weekend. Sometimes I was so groggy I could hardly manage to do a physical examination on a new patient at 3 A.M. I was married but the stipend of forty dollars a month forced us to live in my parents' home. Now that I was a doctor like my father and a possible professional competitor, he argued with me about my diagnoses and treatment and denounced me an incompetent fool. Being called "Doctor" made me feel high and grandiose, partly as a defense against my panic at not knowing what I was doing, and having to deal with life-and-death situations daily.

To flag my sagging self-esteem, I resorted to flirting with

the nurses. Repeating my experiences at Harvard, I was going to be number one by becoming the greatest lover among the intern staff. I started an affair with a rather unattractive student nurse. It was my first episode of infidelity and I was filled with guilt and frightened to death. After all, I loved my wife and did not want to hurt her or lose her. For the first time in my life, I was impotent. The greatest past booster to my self-esteem had failed me. I had a date with the nurse the next evening while a buddy covered for me. She stood me up. I had been bragging about my prowess; now I would be humiliated, a laughing stock among my peers.

The relationship with my father was devastating to me. My anxiety, guilt, and feeling of worthlessness proved overpowering. I felt a total failure in my work and in my love life—another mother had abandoned me. The pain was unbearable. I collected enough barbiturates to kill a horse and took them in my hospital room. The next morning I was discovered and my stomach was pumped but I remained in a coma for ten days. Once again a minor miracle rescued me: Benzedrine had just been discovered and was flown in in time to save me.

No one could any longer ignore this cry for help. I called my analyst. She could not or would not take me, so she referred me to a colleague of hers. He was a soft-spoken, kind man who had been trained at the New York Psychoanalytic Institute, that fortress of classical analysis. There they believed in the use of the couch, patient's sessions four or five times a week, the analyst's impersonal stance and silence, and that almost all psychopathology revolved around the Oedipus complex. This fundamental Freudian tenet— believed to be universal—holds that a person's erotic attraction to the parent of the opposite sex causes fear of castration by the parent of the same sex, and that this is at the root of most neuroses. Through the remainder of my internship, with much cooperation from my fellow interns, I managed to go to analysis four times a week, lie on the couch and talk, and—when I was lucky—get a few sentences at the end of the session from my therapist.

Now it is certainly true that I had Oedipal problems. I remember as a five-year-old child asking my mother to leave my father and run away with me. I certainly felt hatred toward my father, love (perhaps not erotic) toward my mother, many erotic feelings toward my mother's sister, and a gut fear of my father. I had an Oedipus complex a block long. And from my analyst I got Oedipal interpretations more than a block long. But in fact these problems were just a tiny part of the reason for my suicide attempt. What about my perfectionism, my shaky self-esteem, my reaction to abandonment, my grandiosity, my narcissistic wounds? All right, some of these issues had not even been clearly spelled out in analytic theory in 1946. Still, an analyst who was not rigidly wedded to the Oedipus complex as the only central issue would have wondered. In any event, my analyst was a kindly father figure who listened to me and tried his best to help me with my Oedipal problems. My anxiety diminished somewhat. I was able to complete the internship after about six months of analysis and go into residency.

The time with my analyst included the rest of my internship, my residency (another six months) and, after a two-year hiatus for Army service, another year. This was the most rigorous classical analysis I have had.

The classical Freudian theory postulates that if the patient lies on the couch and says whatever comes into his mind (free-associates), what he is unaware of (his unconscious fantasy) will become conscious in the shortest possible time. The analyst is supposed to stay silent for the most part except to interpret instances of resistance and transference. Resistance is an unconscious process that attempts to maintain repression because of the unacceptable nature of the anticipated next revelation. For example, if a patient's repression about his erotic feelings toward his mother or mother-surrogate is about to be lifted, he may begin talking about a movie or baseball game he attended that has no connection to this theme. The analyst at this point needs to point out the patient's digression as an attempt to avoid some more meaningful material without specifying the nature of this repressed material.

Transference is the emergence of irrational attitudes toward the analyst, mostly a repetition of previously held feelings toward some family member. For example, I had feelings of competition toward my analyst, thinking I might have the potential for being a better analyst than he. This was a replay of my competitive feelings with my father and my wanting to be a better doctor than he. So far this sounds pretty reasonable. The only fly in the ointment is that, however silent the analyst tries to be, he cues the patient into what he thinks is important and simultaneously steers the patient away from what he either thinks is unimportant or dreads in himself. The latter is called counterresistance and is one of the most pernicious occurrences in analysis. For example, my therapist felt comfortable dealing with Oedipal material and unknowledgable or uncomfortable or both with other kinds of material. So I "worked out" my Oedipal complex to a fare-thee-well. I gave up "incestuous" attachments, including one to my maternal aunt. I became less fearful of my father, and was able to compete more successfully with men, with less anxiety. But all of my terrors with women, starting with the feelings about abandonment by my mother and sister, were left totally untouched.

While this therapy continued, as I have said, I completed my internship and began my residency in psychiatry. If I had had any doubts about my specialty, my own treatment—with all its deficits that I can now see—had so many positives for me that I decided I wanted to be just like my analyst, a chip off the old block. For one of the first times in my life I had had a relationship with a person who did not criticize me, punish me, or abandon me. I had been listened to, understood (up to a point), and given respect as a person. I certainly did not feel loved or cared about, but these would have been beyond my wildest dreams. I wanted to do for other people in pain at least what this therapist had done for me. Perhaps I could do even more than that. But would my own craziness get in the way? Would my needs and anxieties and insecurity prevent me from being able to help? Was I bright enough? I knew what I wanted to do but was not at all confident that I had either the intellectual or the emotional wherewithal to accomplish it.

4

Residency at a State Hospital and Army Experience

In the late forties the movie called *The Snake Pit,* starring Olivia de Havilland, was released. It depicted in very explicit terms the horrors of the state mental hospitals. To be truthful, the hospital I went to for a six-month residency before my Army service made *The Snake Pit* look good. It was indescribable in its horror. A giant, drab institution about fifty miles from New York City, it probably housed ten thousand patients; they kept coming in but rarely got out alive. Basically it was a custodial institution. Some patients had literally spent their entire adult lives there. One patient I tube-fed daily (she refused to eat) had been tube-fed for twenty years. One week I had to do a vaginal examination on hundreds of patients by order of the state. You can imagine how terrifying this was to a psychotic patient. And you can imagine that I discovered practically no pathology: the examination was so cursory in an attempt to diminish the terror. The hospital was merely complying with a state regulation.

I was the doctor for hundreds of patients. Being the compulsive worker I am, I tried my best to be of some help to at least a few of them, but they were almost all beyond any help. Finally I resigned myself to spending my time doing as much reading in the field as possible. Most of my "work" consisted of signing my name to nurses' reports. The nurses and attendants in general made the ones at Bedlam look good. I am positive there were sexual abuses of female patients as well as sadistic attacks on both men and women.

Patients were lying on the floor naked or half-clothed; wards were crowded and dirty; doctors appeared only for medical emergencies and then only if called by the nurses or attendants. The attendants were often ruffians who treated the patients like animals. Restraints (camisoles, straitjackets) were liberally used. My first assignment was to the female disturbed ward. As I walked through, several women made unfriendly—not erotic—swipes at my genitals. I learned quickly never to turn my back to a patient. A few days after I came onto the ward, a patient walked into the room of another patient who was tied into her bed. The first patient proceeded to enucleate the eye of the restrained patient. Strangely and very mysteriously the sadistic attacker was dead the next day. Yes, this was a "snake pit" all right.

There was no treatment for most patients; such psychotropic drugs as Thorazine had not yet been discovered. There was a small treatment service which had begun to use electric shock therapy on some selected patients. I was not yet allowed to be involved, not even to the degree of being able to observe these treatments. Most of the doctors were refugees, some of whom had not received their license to practice in America. The rest were mostly graduates of foreign medical schools, who did not have the social or cultural contacts to enter private practice. A few were enrolled in analytic institutes and were on their way out of the state system. I was one of the only doctors in my category, a simple resident getting training. I made some friends among the doctors who were enrolled in analytic school. The rest of the doctors were there doing little work, signing a few papers, and getting living quarters, good meals, and a minimum stipend; they were distinguishable from the patients because they carried the keys. Even my first beautiful patient had within two years been transformed into a pasty vegetable by this institution as a result of the alienation caused partly by her schizophrenia and partly by her environment.

Meanwhile, I drove into New York two or three times a

week and continued my own analysis. We decided that it made sense for me to go into the Army and give them the two years I owed them for putting me through medical school during the war. I probably could have gotten out of it on psychiatric deferment, but I decided for a variety of reasons, including a sense of fair play and not wanting my dossier besmirched, to go. In retrospect I realize I should have asked for European service. An Army officer after the war in Europe was treated like a king. However, for reasons of security and familiarity, I chose America and was assigned to Fort Knox, Kentucky.

At Fort Knox I suddenly became a very big fish in a relatively small pond (about ten thousand men). With my six months of "training" at the state hospital, I was the post psychiatrist—the one and only expert for miles around. The post could not operate without me. I had to examine every prisoner, every dischargee, every enlisted man or officer who got into trouble. At Fort Knox I was more important than Freud was in Vienna. There was no competition. The man before me had done a sloppy job and his appointments were backed up for weeks. In my usual compulsive fashion, I worked as hard as was possible (it was a forty-hour work week), but after my internship it seemed practically like a vacation.

During my two-year stint I saw thousands and thousands of people—not only men but also their wives and dependents. I sharpened my diagnostic skills and did as much therapy as was possible, treating people with anxiety and other problems by listening to them and talking to them. Of course, it was a very primitive, unsophisticated, and unsupervised form of therapy, but the sheer numbers and experience were valuable to me. I felt extremely inadequate and insecure about my ability, yet there was no one else the patients could turn to. I certainly learned how to conduct a diagnostic interview and how to feel more comfortable with patients. I had my usual number of erotic countertransferences with patients, but as always kept my feelings well under control. They say, "You never had it so good" about your time in the Army. For me this was probably true. I never had such a short work week in my life; I was given tremendous respect by enlisted men and officers; I learned a great deal; and even though I made only sixty dollars a week, I never lived as well. Officers' clubs, horses, pools, tennis courts, and baseball diamonds were all available to me. I was and continue to be a real sports enthusiast: here were the facilities of my dreams at no cost. Food and supplies were also cheap. I lived better on my sixty dollars a week than I could on six-thousand a week now.

While I was in the Army, I was fortunate in that I was able to attend a weekly seminar in Louisville in neurology with a fine neurologist, one of the most enthusiastic teachers I have encountered. He loved his work, loved to impart knowledge to his students, and was a real performer, charismatic and funny. I really learned neurology backward and forward under him. I have forgotten a great deal, but what I retained has been invaluable in differentiating between certain psychological and neurological problems. These issues come up rarely, but when they do, I feel secure enough to be able to know which patients to refer for neurological investigation. Also under his aegis I had my first professional paper published, on psychomotor epilepsy, an illness in the borderland between the psychological and the organic. This was a big thrill and the first of many papers and later books. While my father in his usual manner disparaged my piece, saying it was only three pages long, I had at last found a way of outdoing him since he had never had a paper published at all.

One day, an alcoholic captain in the medical service corps (not a physician) made a remark about a Russian who had acted badly toward an American. He proceeded to condemn all Russians. I commented: "What does that prove? That the Russians have one asshole in their Army. I think we have a few here, too." He reported this remark of mine to the CIA as evidence that I was a communist. This was 1949, the beginning of the McCarthy era. For three years I was investigated by the FBI, meanwhile being kept out of teaching positions in psychology at the University of Louisville. The FBI checked on contacts I had known in grammar school; people were calling me from all over the country asking what I had done. Finally, after three years, I got a letter from the FBI giving me a clean bill of health. The government had probably spent $100,000 to find out I was not a communist. In fact, I was so apolitical it was almost shocking. Despite being exonerated, this incident increased my suspicion and mistrust of any orthodoxy that restricts freedom of thought or expression and promulgates its own narrow dogma. It probably also had an impact on my psychoanalytic persuasions, since I was less disposed to accept orthodox views. But it didn't make me more political.

My experience in the Army had given me a bit more confidence about my ability to deal with patients. I had been thrown into the breach, the only psychiatrist available, so I could not dwell on invidious comparisons or on my deficiencies. Forced to deal with people in emotional pain, I am sure I did not do brilliantly, but I could see that even with my minimal training and experience I could be helpful. Some of my patients liked me and were grateful for my attempts to help them. I realized that I did have some talent in my work and was encouraged to proceed with it. What the Army experience did for me was to show me I could be in an environment that would accept and respect me. It was "a home away from home" for me, but not like the home I came from. One of my favorite sayings to my patients is "There's no place like home—and thank God for that."

5

Continuing Residency and Beginning Analytic School

When I got back to New York in 1950, I decided to return to Psychiatric Institute to continue my residency. I had been in awe of P.I. when I took my senior elective there and wanted to be in the best possible place for training that would lead to my becoming an analyst. They accepted me at P.I., but there was no salary, so once again we were forced to live with my parents. (Since then residents and interns have been paid enough for minimal subsistence.)

My year of residency at Psychiatric Institute was an important part of my training. I was exposed to the same prominent analysts and learned to think about my patients in a psychoanalytic framework: to think of causes for illness, not merely descriptions. Instead of hundreds of patients, I had six or seven. They were almost all bright, young, and verbal—and I felt sure that they would see through me in a way my patients at Fort Knox could never have done. I was allowed to see them as often as I wished, supervised by a man who had had analytic training. I felt like a member of a special elite group, and, in fact, many of my fellow residents have subsequently made important contributions to the field.

One of my patients was a bright, attractive young woman about my age. I would see her two or three times a week in the same kind of little cubicle I had been in before. Of course, the same kind of feelings arose in me that I had experienced with such patients earlier. I was smitten with her, but—more than that—I had a fantasy that I could establish a deep love and connection to her, not just a sexual one. Once again I feel sure in retrospect that I was attempting unconsciously to revive my lost love with my sister. I found myself dressing up on the days I was scheduled to see her. At one point she commented that she had never seen me in the same outfit twice. I was embarrassed, but decided wisely to cover up my feelings by reverting at that point to being a silent Freudian analyst. In my own analysis I spoke about my feelings for this patient. As would be expected, my therapist focused on the fact that she was a taboo sexual figure (like my mother) rather than on my wish for a deep loving attachment, the sort I had enjoyed and then lost with my sister. In any event, with help from my analyst, I trust I did not do her much harm, even if my countertransference may have prevented me from doing her much good.

During my year at Psychiatric Institute I had learned how to do electric and insulin shock therapy. In those days, as I've said, before the advent of psychotropic medication, that was about all psychiatry had to offer in treating the major psychoses. Laymen often have a great many misapprehensions about electric shock therapy. They feel it is so grisly that it frightens a person out of his psychosis, like the old dunking treatment of the past in which the patient was plunged into the sea. This is not true, although electric shock therapy does look and sound pretty frightening. The patient is tied down, electrodes are put on his head, a current is sent through his brain, and he goes into a grand mal epileptic seizure in which his whole body is in spasms, which lasts exactly forty-five seconds. But the patient feels no pain and is completely unconscious during the seizure, and the treatment is quite safe. In the old days, the convulsive muscular movements would sometimes result in painful musculature or, more rarely, in fractures. However, even in 1950 we were beginning to use muscle relaxants to prevent this. True, there was some mental confusion and memory loss, but this was temporary. Electric shock treatment had an almost miraculous effect in bringing a patient out of an acute schizophrenic break with hallucinations and delusions, or an acute mania or depression in manic-depressive psychosis. It was a godsend to patients in really horrendous psychic pain, suffering from anxiety, persecutory delusions and hallucinations, or feelings of despair. It was misused, to be sure, but it does not deserve the bad name it has with the general public and even with many psychologists and social workers. Nowadays it is used very rarely, having been displaced by medication, which is safer and usually more effective.

In contrast to electric shock therapy, insulin shock therapy was very dangerous and probably totally ineffective. By injecting doses of insulin and sugar, the patient was put into a state shifting between diabetic coma and insulin shock (low blood sugar). He had to be watched at every moment. Death was not frequent, but did occur. And, in fact, though there were some temporary remissions, overall the treatment had little effect on psychoses. It finally ceased to be used.

Another treatment that was somewhat in vogue in the early fifties was lobotomy. Readers may recognize the term from *One Flew Over the Cuckoo's Nest*. Lobotomy, as in that story, was often misused. Technically, it is a surgically refined way of sticking an icepick into the patient's brain over his eyebrow and disrupting certain neuron connections. Even this maligned treatment was of some value in patients who had had every conceivable therapy and were still in constant unremitting psychic torture. However, because of its considerable danger to life, its frequent misuse, and the rare number of situations in which it helped, it fell into deserved disrepute and now is practically never used, even as a last resort.

Although Psychiatric Institute was comparatively very analytically oriented and in fact housed the Columbia Psychoanalytic Institute, the standard American form of thinking about and treating psychiatric patients there and elsewhere in 1950 was to follow the work of Adolf Meyer, an American psychiatrist who has since been virtually forgotten. Meyer's treatment, which he called Psychobiology, was to take a very long, intensive history on the patient and to correlate, with his cooperation and involvement, the external events of his early and later life with his psychiatric symptoms. When I was at Psychiatric Institute, I took these long extensive histories from the patients as well as from their relatives. This approach, connecting background with symptoms, is certainly sound and helpful to some degree. Though Meyer never was interested in unconscious motivation, his method was, in my opinion at least, the best that nonanalytic psychiatry had evolved. It was used throughout our country in the best schools and hospitals. Today, I no longer routinely even take a history on a patient; I let the history come out in pieces connected with the patient's associations. But my Meyerian training was a very good base for me and led naturally into a psychoanalytic frame since both agree on the idea of psychic determinism, cause and effect.

While finishing my residency at Psychiatric Institute, I began applying to psychoanalytic institutes. Psychoanalysis—which was what I longed now to study and use—dealt with cause and effect, with psychodynamics as opposed to organic or behavioral treatment. The method was "talking," but in contrast to the Meyerian approach, the aim was to penetrate the unconscious. The rest of psychiatry I had come to realize was relatively pedestrian and not intellectually challenging. The number one institute in terms of prestige was the New York Psychoanalytic—that super-rigid bastion of classical Freudian psychoanalysis (about which Janet Malcolm has written recently). I decided that in applying, I would neglect to mention my two suicide attempts.

In those days there were tremendously rigid criteria in choosing candidates. For example, no homosexual could be admitted, and people with a good deal of personal psychopathology—like myself—tended to be excluded. I had three interviews with some of the pundits of the New York Psychoanalytic. One remains in my memory. I came into a dimly lit office and sat down. The interviewer said, "Tell me something about yourself." I talked nonstop for an hour and a half without his saying a word. When I paused to catch my breath, he smiled sweetly and said, "Why don't you tell me something about yourself?" The result of my interviews was that I was rejected by the New York Psychoanalytic Institute. Now this may sound like sour grapes and perhaps it is to some degree. After all, I had not been rejected by many institutions in my life. However, I cannot say how happy I am today that I was rejected by New York Psychoanalytic and chosen by the analytic school at the Flower-Fifth Avenue Hospital. I do not think I could have accepted the orthodoxy at the New York Psychoanalytic; probably I would have rebelled and left.

When I left Psychiatric Institute, I was not only allowed but encouraged to take as many patients as I could to start a private practice. Private practice was much more frightening than working either in the Army or in a hospital. My patients were now *my* personal responsibility. I had no organization or supervisor to whom I could pass the buck. Their lives were in my hands—and I was terrified. Every single night, I would go over my work with my patients and beat myself (as my grandfather would have) for every mistake I had made. And at the beginning the mistakes were plentiful. My self-criticism certainly helped me to grow as a therapist, but my self-flagellation was excessive, painful, and unproductive. A beginning therapist, even without a grandfather like mine, goes through the tortures of the damned. He knows he has an awesome responsibility to his patients and he feels totally inadequate to understand them and meet their emotional needs. Being helpless to deal with a patient's pain is excruciating.

Even with my first private patients I could not adhere to the "rules" of treating patients. I do not see how I could have followed the standards of silence and nonparticipation laid down by the New York Psychoanalytic Institute. In any

33

event, I had also applied to the analytic school connected with the New York Medical College—Flower and Fifth Avenue Hospitals. (In the business, it is called "Flower.") This school could in no way prevent dissent or insist on adherence to dogma. Most of the faculty had at one time been members of the American Psychoanalytic Association (the national organization) and had left because of theoretical disagreements with the classical position. Some of them still adhered to the basic Freudian ideas, but with modifications and a good deal of flexibility. The other group at Flower, which we called the "culturalists," had split more openly from the Freudian model and followed analysts like Karen Horney and Clara Thompson, who stressed social and cultural factors in the etiology of neurosis.

Both of these theorists had largely dismissed the unconscious and focused instead on the influence of the society on the development of character. Horney especially focused her work on the analysis of character. She attacked such character defenses as neurotic pride, idealized self, resignation, and self-effacement; and she dealt with the patient's attitudes toward himself and others. All this is quite a long way from sex or instincts or the Oedipus complex. So, with a faculty consisting of those two opposing factions they could hardly insist on dogma. In fact, as I slowly began to realize, the "culturalists" in my institute were almost a kind of "cell" (as McCarthy would have called it) within the faculty. Since many or most of them were or had been devoted communists or socialists, they had to find some way of making psychoanalysis fit with communism. This was no easy task. Although there was a school of Marxist psychoanalysis, psychoanalysis is forbidden today in communist countries. In China, for example, psychiatric problems are dealt with by reeducation in communist philosophy. In any event, the culturalists at Flower in one way or another sought to find the root of neurotic problems in the capitalist society in which we live.

I have no doubt that our system does produce a great

many neurotic conflicts. The emphasis on production, the encouragement of greed, the threat of war and the arms race, the dehumanization of the factory or the corporation, the difference between our stated moral values and what is really required for survival certainly take their toll on our psyche. But perhaps because I am so apolitical, I do not see much that I as an analyst can do about society in general. I think a politician might have a better shot at changing things than I (though not a very good shot at that). I do think it is important to be aware of the influence of society on us, including our ethnicity. I think it is important to help a patient understand how these social forces have shaped him and to encourage him to express his individuality despite pressures to conform. However, I still feel that the specifics of our childhood experience have an even greater impact on us than does our society. So with my analyst as my internalized role model, I joined the Freudian wing of the school (we all were exposed to the same courses) and became a leading warrior against the culturalists. And I fear my own insecurity made me move in the direction of rigidity and overcertainty in my beliefs.

When I entered Flower in 1951, I had to leave my current analyst and go into treatment with someone on their faculty. I picked a man who had been warm, pleasant, and friendly when I went to him for my initial interviews for the school. My new analyst was certainly the antithesis of a rigid analyst. But he was a wonderful example of how a *lack* of discipline and restraint can render an analyst almost totally ineffective. Here I was in a school which had a relatively small faculty and student body. One quality that is not only imperative but the lack of which is actually illegal is confidentiality. My analyst was a "yenta" and a blabbermouth. Throughout my sessions he would often "badmouth" other students in treatment with him or faculty members; naturally, I assumed—I am sure correctly—that he would do the same about me. Furthermore, during my sessions his girlfriend would walk in and out of the room freely, as did a gay man who may or may not have been his lover as well. I got a bit miffed when, sitting behind the couch, he would watch the Army-McCarthy hearings on television, though I had to admit they were probably a good deal more interesting. In one session he was walking around the room while I lay on the couch. "Quick, Dick," he beckoned, looking out of the window, "Catch the ass on that broad across the street!" In another, he was on the phone practically the whole time: "Diabetic coma . . . immediate hospitalization . . . looks bad." Again I was rather annoyed about my whole session, for which I was paying dearly, going down the tubes. However, a medical emergency could not be disregarded. "Who was it?" I asked solicitously. "Oh, that was my dog," he replied.

As part of my "treatment" he asked to see my wife, whom I had foolishly but correctly described as an extraordinarily beautiful woman. Well, in a little while, he wanted to see more and more of her. Hearing she was also a gourmet cook, he asked her to cook for him. This was all part of a "training analysis"—an analysis intended not only to purify me but to serve as a model of technique. When the good doctor did offer interpretations or remarks—and he did so often—they were totally off the mark, reflecting his own rather than my problems. I spoke to fellow candidates who had had the same kind of experience with him. He was so totally narcissistic and undisciplined, he made what could have been a Marx Brothers or Mel Brooks parody of our analyses.

Another habit of his we soon learned was that, if a student left him to transfer to another analyst, he would blackball him and prevent his graduating. The three or four unfortunates in my class who went to him decided there was nothing we could do except stick it out with him for the three years of school and then go off and get a real analysis. He was unique; the other analysts on the faculty were responsible and mature.

The material in analytic school, in contrast to my per-

sonal analytic experience, really turned me on. I read pro-
fusely many important books in psychoanalysis. Since I
had simultaneously started my private practice, I had a reference point for all the theory I learned. One of the good
things that came from my analyst's being such a blabbermouth was that he told me in my senior year (against all the
rules of the school) that my average on the written examinations on analytic theory over the three years was a perfect
100 percent. That really pleased me. And this time I was
doing it not for my grandfather but for myself. To me there
can be no subject as engrossing as the search for the meaning of life. Everything I read on psychoanalytic theory was
part of this search. But reading about it in the abstract can
often be boring. Applying it every day to treating a patient
makes it come alive. I never had to force myself to study,
as I had done in every other situation, including medical
school. Of course, I was studying material I had been interested in since high school. This was not forced labor but a
dream come true.

My control analyses were as spectacularly good as my
training analysis was bad. By "control analysis," we mean a
very careful supervision by the training analyst of the patients we are treating. We had to follow two patients for a
year, reporting verbatim what the patients said and what we
said. Then the two training analysts told us what we should
have said, which was frequently quite different! One of my
training analysts was Bernard Glueck, who must have been
in his seventies when he supervised me. He knew so much
about the unfolding of the unconscious that he could literally predict what the patient's major trend in the following
session would be. He gave me a solid grounding in the
science of psychoanalysis. If the next session can be pre-
dicted, then we must be dealing with a science. To give an
example within a familiar Oedipal context, if I am dealing
with a patient's competitiveness with his father and his wish
to defeat him, then I can expect that he (as I had) might
have a dream or associations dealing with a fear that his

father may castrate him. If I know what to expect in the subsequent session, I can be selectively attentive to the patient's concerns about his physical health or possibilities of injury. These may be precursors to more direct material about castration anxiety.

There *are* certain theories postulated by Freud that cannot be ignored. We know that there is an unconscious, an area of the mind that is out of the awareness of the person. If a suitable climate can be set up in which the patient feels the analyst will be interested, caring, nonjudgmental, and will maintain confidentiality at all costs, then there will be an orderly unfolding of the unconscious material. The analyst's main role is to interpret resistance and transference. If the analyst deviates from his position as an observer and listener, he must be responsible for understanding the impact of his deviation in technique. On this last point, I agree; but I gave, and continue to give myself a great deal more leeway than almost any other analyst I knew. For instance, I not infrequently have contacts with patients outside of my office. (I will have more to say on this later on.)

Accepting the science of psychoanalysis immediately rules out humanistic and existential analysts, who respond to what *they*—not the patient—feel at the moment. I am a strong believer in using my feelings in response to the patient's material and in deviating a great deal from the blank screen model. But I like to think that I never gave up my scientific base. I do not introduce my own feelings or problems for my own sake, but only in response to the patient. My training analyst was an important negative role model for my doing so and Dr. Glueck a positive one. He was a somewhat gruff old fellow, basically good-hearted, but he did not countenance any nonsense. Luckily for me, in terms of the learning process, the patient I was reporting on was one toward whom I had the most outrageous erotic countertransference. In one session, the manifest or surface content was a discussion of whether she should use the couch, as she was currently sitting up. The latent, or hidden, content was my sexual interest in her and a kind of seduction on her part by playing coy. I was too inexperienced and too blind to understand. Dr. Glueck banged on his desk and said in his German accent: "Thees ees not psychoanalysis; thees ees lovemaking!"

My other control analysis was with Dr. William V. Silverberg, who was a very erudite and prominent analyst whom I was to go to later for my personal analysis when I ended the treatment with my analyst. Silverberg, too, was extremely scientific, and he indoctrinated me with so much basic structure that later on I was free to deviate from it without losing it altogether, as my training analyst had. An analyst's first supervision can have a tremendous impact on his development. One of the areas of my work I feel most proud of is that I have taught and supervised hundreds of young analysts and had a share in their development. The case on which I was supervised by Dr. Silverberg was that of a lesbian who came into treatment not because she wished to change her sexual preference, but because of headaches, anxiety, insomnia, and interpersonal difficulties. During her treatment, mainly through dream analysis, the dynamics of her homosexuality became conscious. Without my willing her to do so or her forcing herself because of social compliance, or compliance to my wishes as her analyst, she became heterosexual. A thirty-year follow-up has shown that she never once returned to lesbianism. Treating this kind of patient is difficult for an experienced analyst— and I was only a beginner. She was one of my first private patients. I wrote up the case history, dedicating it to Dr. Silverberg, and this became my first book, *Voyage from Lesbos*.

I had decided to finish my residency training at New York University–Bellevue and to specialize in child psychiatry there. In retrospect, I cannot really understand my reasons for the choice (perhaps to understand better my own childhood), but it proved to be an interesting one. The chief of the service was probably the best known child psychiatrist in the country. She was a very gruff, direct woman in her fifties named Loretta Bender. The children's ward at Bellevue was really a zoo. Of course, Bellevue Psychiatric was much the same as the state hospital had been. But this was a teaching hospital connected with a medical school. The ward was filled with autistic children—children in a world of their own—and hyperactive ones. Dr. Bender did not believe in psychotherapy of any kind. She basically thought that all psychiatric disorders, including neuroses, were organic. So she was happily and busily giving electric shock treatments to children as young as five—and unfortunately it was sometimes my turn to apply the electrodes and push the button. This was not my most pleasant task as a resident.

I certainly learned a lot about children and also how to distinguish between psychogenic and organic illnesses. For example, I interviewed many parents of children who were diagnosed either as autistic or schizophrenic. These parents were no different than most; the diseases, ergo, must be organic rather than caused by environment, as Dr. Bender believed. Actually, she was not too far off as far as the population that she saw went. But you can imagine how disturbed a child must be before his parents let him come to Bellevue. Bender's mistake was that she generalized from the particular. Many of the patients she saw were in fact organic. Their disease was caused by brain damage—genetic or intrauterine. But there is no way I or anyone else would now believe all psychiatric problems were organic. And even if they were, shock treatment for five-year-olds was a bit much!

During my last year of Bellevue and while I was building up my private practice, one of the things I undertook in an attempt to support myself (my costs included my own analysis, my control analyses with Silverberg and Glueck, and—just to make things complete—my wife's analysis) was to administer electric shock therapy for a Dr. David Impastato. He was a kindly, wise man, who admitted he had little interest in psychotherapy, but gave shock treatment to many of the patients he saw. Some mornings I would do the shock therapy for him. He might very easily make fifty dollars each on the thirty or forty patients I treated; I got the handsome sum of fifty dollars for my morning's work. But I also saw some of his patients for psychotherapy, and again he got the lion's share of the fee. I was presented with the patients, his nurse did the collecting, and I used his office. I am not denigrating the good doctor. I understood the contract and it benefitted me as well as him.

I remember one morning I was supposed to give a shock treatment to a patient in her late fifties. The night before the treatment I was filled with anxiety and something in me told me not to treat her. I had taken a history and done a thorough physical examination and there were no obvious abnormalities; perhaps there were some signs that were so minimal they did not even reach my consciousness. In any event, I insisted she have an electrocardiagram before the treatment. It showed extensive heart damage. She did not receive the shock treatment, but she died of a heart attack two weeks later. There is no doubt she would have died during the treatment if I had administered it. I have learned to trust my intuition and to use my anxiety as an index that I may be moving in a dangerous direction. Sometimes anxiety can be an index of health rather than psychopathology.

The early years of private practice were incredibly difficult. I spent much of my spare time criticizing myself for my mistakes, aware that my patients would be better off with a more experienced therapist. I did not know whether experience would really make me "good enough." And I had all those analysts to pay; my practice was growing but still small. I had to work as a resident during the day some of the time. I had analytic school two or three nights a week plus a mountain of reading. I even took my specialty boards in psychiatry right after completing my residency. On Sunday mornings I had to take a course to sharpen up on the details of neurology, much of which I had proceeded to forget.

I saw my patients in a room in my parents' home. This was not an unmixed blessing, but who could afford an office? Through part of that time I was forced to live in my parents' house with my wife and two children. At this time I had taken in all the admonitions about the importance of anonymity, yet here my patients were constantly running into my father, hardly an unobtrusive man. He had his office on the first floor and I on the second and we shared a waiting room. Often my mother would serve as secretary and receptionist for my father. I was constantly trying to keep my wife (hardly unobtrusive either because of her beauty) and my children, aged from one to three and five to seven in these years, from making any noise and being visible to my patients.

I am sure it did not work and my patients were well aware of my family. But I am equally sure that the anonymity of the analyst is mostly a paranoid protection of himself rather than a therapeutic bonus. When I went to my first bona fide analyst, he had a system whereby a patient came in one door and out another. One day I was late, only to discover that the patient preceding me had been a classmate of mine in medical school. And, of course, I knew absolutely nothing personal about my analyst. My training analyst was another story—but to what a degree!

One can also imagine the effect that all this work, being thrown in with Mom & Pop, and my never being home had on my family life. To put it very mildly, it was not helpful. I had an enormous emotional need from putting out so much energy in my work and being so self-critical. There was very little time to fill my needs and repair my wounded self-image at home, and I had very little left to give to my wife and children. "I gave at the office." So home was hardly what it should have been. I was needy, demanding, short-tempered, obsessed with my work, and had little energy to be loving or caring. How my wife and children survived it all is beyond me; in fact, I do not think any of them survived this period very well.

My first patient in private practice was a man I took with me from Psychiatric Institute, though he was treated by one of my colleagues while there. At the first session, I began to understand why my colleague had been so generous in turning him over to me. He was a very angry young man in his middle twenties. Violence was just beneath the surface. He came up to the second floor of my parents' home. My office had been the library in their home, and it contained many paintings, including an original by Vasari, the Renaissance historian. The patient sat down and without a word presented me with a picture he had done. In the center in capital letters was the word "HATE." Around it were mutilated bodies covered with red blood.

For me this was certainly a baptism by fire. This poor young man was filled with hatred, trusted no one—which was certainly reasonable from his childhood experience—and was challenging me. He was paranoid, he was schizophrenic, and he was also homosexual. There were some patients like him at Psychiatric Institute and I had to take anyone I could get into my practice. Though I had learned something about the Oedipus complex and repression and dream analyses from my courses, my supervisors, and my reading, I wondered how they would help me deal with him. I threw all of that knowledge out, decided to break all the rules, and attempted to be warm, kind, and empathic with him. This was not false; it was authentic. "Authentic" is a big word with me—and I don't mean it in a fashionable "California" sense. I don't think a therapist should ever be anything but genuine with a patient. He should never lie by omission or commission. By this I am not implying that he should always say to the patient what he feels at the moment he feels it. But he should never deny to himself a feeling he has—even a very negative feeling—but should try to examine first by himself or with a colleague or supervisor, and then, if appropriate, with the patient, what in the patient brought out this feeling in him. That is not to say the patient bears the total responsibility. The analyst has his own psychopathology. We are dealing with a two-part transaction. Some people who drive others crazy do not affect me adversely; others who may be inoffensive to most may make me furious. It depends how they connect with my past.

In any event, Joe did not make me crazy or even frighten me. I could easily relate to the hurt child in him. So, after a while of breaking down some of the major elements in his mistrust, I decided the only way of getting across to him that there might be someone in this world who would not despise or reject him was to invite him to dinner with my family and to go to the ballet, one of his favorite entertainments, with him. This was more effective than a million interpretations would have been. It was a concrete act of acceptance—and it worked. Joe loosened up, got warm and friendlier, and became less paranoid and hostile. I am sure I did not cure him, but I am equally sure I was an important figure in his life. Just as my first bona fide analyst was the first person to accept me, I represented this for Joe, more than a doctor.

I think that an analyst should always respond first as a human being, then as a doctor, and finally as an analyst. Many analysts, I fear, have the order reversed. An analyst should share a patient's joy or sorrow before he analyzes the reason for it. I regularly go to the weddings or bar mitzvahs and other important joyous events of my patients and their children. I have also spent an entire weekend with a patient when her husband died. If a patient brings in some good news that is a culmination of a sincere effort, we will often embrace, and there are also embraces that signify the sharing of a tragic event or loss. There is no reason why an analyst should hide his genuine feeling self. This does not interfere with analysis; it enhances it. The patient can feel a genuine trust and will be free to reveal more of himself and his unconscious.

The notion that this kind of genuine human feeling on the part of the analyst "dilutes the transference" is, in my view, nonsense. The proponents of this theory say, of course, that unless the analyst is a blank screen, the patient's realistic view of him will interfere with the projection onto him of various figures from the patient's past. I must admit this sounds reasonable. However, I do not feel it is true. I cannot prove this, but it has been my clinical experience that these transferences occur even when patients know a great deal about me. And lately some very classical analysts such as Ralph Greenson have written that the more solid the realistic relationship with the analyst is, the more trust is established, and the easier it is for the patient to bring out his most horrendous aspects and to project them or the more significant figures of his past onto the analyst. My human approach has hardly prevented me from being the recipient of the most vicious primitive attacks from the most intact civilized patients, who were obviously transferring to me feelings about early childhood figures.

The second response—after the human one—is *to be a doctor*. To be a doctor means to have the awesome responsibility of a person's life in your hands, perhaps even more than if you were a surgeon or an internist. Their mistakes can kill, but yours can lead to a lifetime of suffering. Being a doctor to me means being always on call. I am disgusted with modern physicians who refuse to make house calls; if the situation calls for it, I make house calls. And I also decry those analysts who refuse calls from patients. My patients know I am always on call twenty-four hours a day. That is one good quality I learned from my father, who held this view and acted on it. When I am away, I make sure I am covered by doctors of the same persuasion as myself. Also, my itinerary is always available. I have received calls from patients while in Jamaica and in England. Does this infantalize the patient? I think not. Very few patients avail themselves of my availability. When a patient abuses the privilege—which is almost unheard of with my patient population—this is grist for the analytic mill; something to be discussed in the treatment.

"Being a doctor," however, means more than being available. In any context, including dancing with a patient at her son's bar mitzvah, it involves a need not to suspend the awareness that a patient has put her life in your hands. This means you have a special relationship with the person, different from almost any other one. It means you have to be very careful not to abuse the power that has been given you, for it is very easy for doctors to do so. Of course, I have run into many many cases of doctors' abuse of patients; sometimes it is sexual, sometimes it is financial. But many times—and far more frequently—it is much more subtle. For example, if a doctor is attracted to a patient of his and does not actually engage in any sexual activity but enjoys the mutual seduction without analyzing it, he is abusing his position by allowing this mutual "love affair" to continue interminably. So no matter what the manifest situation is with a patient, I must never forget that I am her doctor and I have a deep responsibility to care for her welfare, a responsibility I have toward no other person except perhaps a young child of mine.

The third level of response, that of the analyst, must also never be dropped for a moment. Everything that goes on with a patient must be grist for the analytic mill. So if I play tennis with a patient—which I have done not infrequently— and he is unable to defeat me despite superior skills, then we must analyze whether this is because he is afraid to compete with his father. There are certain patients at certain stages of treatment that I would not see outside of the office: for instance, if the patient were in the process of trying to separate from me emotionally. I might not play tennis with someone who was in a very competitive transference with me. In any event, whenever I have dinner or go to a party with a patient, I always have to check out what their reactions were to me or my companion. These are often very valuable clues as to transference reactions.

To explain the ability to deviate from rules, I am reminded of the book *Zen and the Art of Archery*. This describes how a person must learn how to shoot a bow and arrow compulsively for seven years before he can let go and do it without thinking, without fear of getting out of control. My years of experience and getting some of my countertransference possibilities into my consciousness have reinforced this conviction. I now know in what directions I am apt to stray, so that I have better, although by no means perfect, ways of checking these. My background of compulsive indoctrination by my grandfather probably allowed me the liberty of letting go without the fear of going too far. After all, how many five-year-olds refuse to go to kindergarten because it is not hard enough work? And my father as a doctor did not take a day off, including Sunday, in the first thirty years of his practice and would literally "walk miles through the snow" to visit a sick patient. Their incorporations may have made me a compulsive, unhappy person, but they also allowed me certain privileges I certainly do not advise others with dissimilar psyches to take. I can be surer that I will not stray, as my training analyst did. In effect, the American Psychoanalytic Association, the bastion of classical psychoanalysis, is a latterday grandfather for many of its students. Perhaps applied at that time of their life, it does more than instill structure; it destroys initiative and creativity. Then, thinking about it, my grandfather always encouraged me to write poetry and prose and to come up with new ideas. He wanted me to work constantly, but he did not discourage and in fact greatly encouraged my creativity. He wanted me to be a leader and an outstanding professional.

My grandfather, however, was not the only influence in choosing a technique (that hated word "technique," which implies a way of dealing with situations that is prefabricated and applied universally). My "technique" is to be spontaneous and authentic, once it is understood that I have the responsibilities as a human being and as a doctor, and once I have stated that I have incorporated a knowledge of theory as an analyst. Another obvious influence on me was the lack of any warm, intimate, empathic communication from either my parents or grandparents. The only taste of this I had in my childhood was from my sister. For this reason, I was left with a craving for closeness. I am never threatened by a woman's engulfing me, only by her possible abandonment of me. And I never had enough or too much closeness with patients. Most of my colleagues and patients had intensive, smothering "Jewish mothers," whether or not they were in fact Jewish. They marvel at my insatiability and desire for closeness. Perhaps that was why the whole business of the analyst behind the couch came into being. Freud admitted he could not stand looking at patients all day long, but, of course, the fascinating point is that Freud had a Jewish mother! If Freud had been Italian, he might have held every patient in his arms. I have not done that with most patients, but I have on those occasions on which it seemed an appropriate human response.

It seems to me that each analyst must find a way of doing therapy that evolves out of his personal history and his personality. It would be just as incorrect for me to try to get everyone to do analysis my way as it has been to rigidify the "technique" to do it Freud's way. In fact, of course, Freud did not conduct therapy at all as the so-called Freudian model suggests. People who were in therapy with him recall that he was infinitely more informal than his followers. One of his patients remembered that on one occasion he (the patient) analyzed a dream of his own according to a paper Freud had written. "No, no," objected Freud. "But that was exactly what your paper said," remarked the patient. "You're right," said Freud, "but I just wrote that paper to pass the time one rainy afternoon. It's nonsense!"

We know that Freud took many of his patients along with him when he went to the mountains on vacation. All this is really to point out once again that an analyst's style should grow out of his own self. Imposing a style is similar to getting an artist to paint by giving him a coloring book. In short, I believe that is what killed the art and the creativity in Freudian psychoanalysis, and what has made so many analysts and their patients zombies. It is really *1984*.

Another childhood influence that affected the way I worked and my personal style with patients was my relationship with my father. He always presented himself as *the* most skilled, dedicated, and successful doctor; indeed, in his circle of Italo-American doctors, he was among the most successful. He was the president of the medical board at Columbus Hospital but was so competitive and so destructive to his colleagues that he received "poison pen" letters and finally resigned. It is no wonder; he would openly call almost every one of his colleagues an incompetent charlatan, a knave, and a thief. Well, I had received a comparable attack from him, appropriate to my level of development. When I received my specialty boards in psychiatry, he commented that I might have some book knowledge, but I would never be able to deal with people who had problems anywhere near as well as he could. My father was not subtle; he was right out there.

Having spent several hundreds of thousands of dollars resolving my Oedipal problem, I realized that there were only two choices. I had either to let him castrate me and submit to him, or beat him at his own game and thus destroy him. In analysis I had a dream in which I had appendicitis and he was the surgeon performing the appendectomy. The knife slipped and he cut my testicles off. The only way to cut *his* off would be to supplant him as the best, most dedicated, most successful doctor in the world. When he was dying and I confronted him with the fact that he had never given me any respect for my professional achievements, he said that the only way I could ever earn his respect would be to become professor of psychiatry at Harvard Medical School. I explained to him that what I did was infinitely more creative—I was teaching seasoned professionals, not medical students. I told him I would not take that job if they paid me a million dollars a year; I literally would not. He turned his head away and said, "You asked how you could gain my respect. I told you."

In any case, I had to beat him at his own game. I had to work harder, be even more available to my patients, become even more skilled at my work. I had to do the equivalent of walking three miles through the snow to save a sick child. (Once during a snowstorm I literally walked several miles through the snow to reach my office.) So my compulsive need to defeat my father as a better doctor has also been a driving force that has affected my style as an analyst. I do not attribute my commitment to my sterling character. In some other areas of my life—my relationship to my children, for instance—I have been far from sterling. But my childhood and adult experience helped mold the kind of person and the kind of analyst I became. This is true of all analysts. Indeed, to cast them all in the same mold would destroy their individuality and their effectiveness.

6

Early Years in Private Practice

During my early years in private practice in the fifties, I made an attempt to be more of a Freudian analyst. In truth, this was easier for me then because I was relatively cut off from intimacy except to gratify my needs. Some of my patients, but a relatively small percentage, I put on the couch. I was as silent and anonymous as I could stand being, although nothing like the Freudians. I rarely saw patients more than once or twice a week. I felt then, and continue to feel, that seeing patients more frequently is for the benefit of the analyst more than the patient. This procedure makes it much easier for the analyst to follow the patient and ensures his income with fewer patients. Using the couch allows him to daydream and retreat into his own fantasy while relaxing behind it. The problem caused by this "technique" is that it sets up a situation fraught with rules that prevent any spontaneous emotional interaction.

The technique therefore also protects the analyst against any real emotional involvement, which would drain and perhaps upset him. He and the patient play a prescribed little game in which neither gets involved in anything emotional, except that the patient has some psychodramatic transference experiences, which both of them know are part of the game. Because of the setting, even those experiences often do not have any real impact. I have done second or third analyses so many times with patients who went through this process, got somewhat less anxious temporarily, but resolved very little. In fact, I myself was one of those patients, though in truth I did become able to defeat my father rather than succumb to him. However, I was still quite cut off from intimate interactions.

Even in the fifties, in listening to my patients with what I like to believe was an open mind, I found that many if not most of their problems were pre-Oedipal. Their issues had a great deal to do with disturbances in the mother–child relationship in the first years of life. During the latter half of the fifties I had two papers published on such instances. In both situations I was merely reporting the progress of a patient. One of the papers was a case report entitled "The Importance of Trauma During the First Year of Life." A young fellow in his twenties came to see me because he had made a serious suicide attempt when he thought his girlfriend had rejected him; in addition to this he was enuretic—a bedwetter. The patient was a remarkably intact, mature, happy fellow. He seemed to have no particular Oedipal problems around the issue of competition, being assertive but not compulsively so. He liked his work and did very well at it. He appeared to have two relatively loving parents with whom he had a good relationship. Yet this fellow would surely have been dead but for fortunate circumstances. He lay down on a busy highway at night expecting to be run over. How come a person who was so intact could have this island of very severe, life-destroying pathology?

I decided to ask his mother to come in. She seemed a loving, caring, interested mother, without being either intrusive or possessive; if there were only more mothers like her, I would be out of business. So what happened? In analyzing the patient's dreams, he had reported instances of tremendous deprivation of his oral or nurturing needs. His dreams pointed out that he had enormous rage at an abandoning feeding figure, a rage so great that his only way to prevent murder was suicide: turning this rage against himself. Finally we postulated that the patient must have been subjected early in his life to a life-threatening deprivation. When he got in touch with his anger, his depression was diminished and his enuresis subsided. I asked him to check with his mother to see if he could find some instance of early separation from her due to an illness of his or hers. Instead, he reported that during the first weeks of life his mother's milk had become thin and he had nearly died before the situation was discovered. This brought about the anger that was expressed as suicide when he thought his current mother-surrogate was abandoning him. It also accounted for the enuresis as an unconscious expression of anger at his mother.

I want to point out that the patient recovered *before* he verified this data by checking with his mother on his experience as an infant. Also, after his working through these issues, he discovered that his girlfriend had been unfaithful to him. Even this did not bring about a return of his symptoms. In fact, follow-up confirmed that he married her and had no further symptoms. All these miraculous events took place in less than a year of seeing him once a week. Granted this was an extraordinary case. Obviously, too, I was very tuned in to the patient because his pathology was so close to my own. The difference was that he had one isolated area of trouble whereas mine spread across most areas of my life. This brings us to the oft quoted but valid joke that "You don't have to be crazy to be a psychiatrist, but it helps." The fact that I have experienced such a wide range of psychic traumata certainly makes me more sensitive to those of others.

To return to my sensitivity to pre-Oedipal trauma, Freud had certainly written about the issues that arise in the first year of life. Among his followers, Karl Abraham in Europe and later Bertram Lewin in Pittsburgh had written brilliant essays on the subject. So it is not that this material was not available to American psychoanalysts; it is just that they were "selectively inattentive" to it. That wonderful phrase was coined by the American psychoanalyst Harry Stack Sullivan, who also was one of the first to suggest that the analyst should be a "participant observer" rather than a mere observer in the process of analysis, that the analyst should communicate responses to the patient and be involved in the process of therapy.

Actually at this time there were many English and Latin-American analysts whose major focus was on the early mother–child dyad, the pre-Oedipal period. Unfortunately, I did not become seriously acquainted with their work until ten years later. These analysts, some of whom I shall discuss later, include Melanie Klein, W. Ronald D. Fairbairn, Hanna Segal, Donald W. Winnicott, Harry Guntrip, and John Bowlby (all English), and Heinrich Racker from Argentina. I am obviously choosing the names that have had the most impact on me out of many who have made significant contributions. Interestingly, I was paralleling much of their thinking without, of course, even beginning to match their genius, and before knowing anything about their work. In fact, I was one of the first analysts I know of in America to "discover" them and write about them.

One of the most important reports I undertook, which involved a great many of these first-year-of-life issues, was my first book, *Voyage from Lesbos,* which arose out of the patient I presented to Dr. William V. Silverberg for one of my control analysis cases. This patient's treatment was on the couch and almost exclusively through dream analysis. The patient was a prolific dreamer. The material that came out in her analysis largely through dreams dealt in the main with her relationship to her mother during the early years of her life. Parenthetically, I might point out that in the fifties both male and female homosexuality was looked upon— even in the analytic community—as some strange deviation that had to be stamped out. Now, I am certainly not, and never was, one of those analysts who thinks of homosexuality as a disease; in fact, this patient is one of the very few homosexual patients I have treated who changed her sexual preference. So, this patient was quite unusual. The point I am trying to make here is that what was really remarkable about my work with this patient was not her "cure," but rather what I learned from this patient about the importance of the relationship to the mother in the early years of life.

After finishing the book, I dedicated it to Dr. Silverberg, who was kind enough to write me a very fine introduction. And as soon as I graduated from analytic school, I left my training analyst and went to Dr. Silverberg for analysis, this time sitting up. "I've been on my back too long—in more ways than one," I told him. Silverberg was a brilliant, intellectual, impeccable, analytically precise therapist. He was an excellent dream analyst and I was a prolific dreamer. We plunged into depths in my unconscious. But Silverberg, too, was in general "selectively inattentive" to early mother–child issues. I am sure in retrospect that this was connected with a counterresistance—an inability on his part to deal with those issues himself. And, of course, *his* analyst's inability to do so. But within these limitations, my analysis with him on the issues he did deal with was excellent: "impeccable" is the word that again comes to mind. He was a flawless, disciplined technician with a fine reputation. He treated many "celebrities." The patient who followed me into his office was Montgomery Clift, one of my favorite actors.

In my analysis with Silverberg, some of what we went over again was my Oedipal problem and my need to defeat my father. Silverberg had a male secretary. As part of my emasculating him, I would accuse him of being homosexual and living with his secretary. He dealt with this material flawlessly—never acknowledging or denying the truth of this because, in fact, it was totally irrelevant to my treatment. I do not feel self-revelation on the part of the analyst is always the correct procedure for every patient, and I myself am certainly not always automatically self-revealing. It never occurred to me or concerned me that Silverberg might in fact be homosexual, although to be a homosexual analyst in the late fifties was a complete anathema.

Imagine my surprise when after his death, it was revealed

that Silverberg was, in fact, a homosexual. My fantasies had not been far afield. But more shocking still, because he was such a meticulous analyst, was the fact that he had apparently been in love with Montgomery Clift while Clift was his patient. He had even inscribed his book *Childhood Experience and Personal Destiny* to Clift, "To my hero." Apparently Silverberg's countertransference had a disastrous effect on Clift, who sank deeper and deeper into drugs and alcohol without being able to be rescued. Two separate biographies of Clift put a great deal of the blame on Silverberg for not taking more direct and decisive action in hospitalizing him and for keeping him as an analytic patient despite his obvious deterioration. I have no contempt or negative judgment toward Silverberg, only deep sympathy for what must have been a terrible net in which he was caught. He was a man of such character and such integrity that his plight must have been excruciating to him.

One can certainly understand that he must have made a very serious error in continuing to treat Clift while he was in love with him and Clift was deteriorating. Clearly, he was emotionally trapped—and Clift had the kind of charisma almost in a league with Marilyn Monroe. Both men and women were drawn to his need and his vulnerability. His problems undoubtedly went back to his very early life, yet Silverberg apparently could deal neither with Clift's problems nor his own or mine when it came to that area. I remember hearing Silverberg present a case report on Clift to our analytic society on one occasion. I was a bit shocked because Clift could easily be recognized (by me, for instance) and this was a flagrant violation of the rule of confidentiality with a nationally known figure. It must have been part of Silverberg's countertransference, or an attempt to get responses from peers to help him deal with it. Ordinarily he was so punctilious and proper about such matters. Of course I am sure he had Clift's permission to present a paper on him, just as I had my patient's to write a book about her. Still, without his countertransference, Silverberg would never have exposed confidential material on such a prominent person, practically a legend in and after his time. My patient, by contrast, was an unknown secretary who after a few attempts to disguise her was not even recognizable from the book to some of her friends.

The Silverberg–Clift situation points out how vulnerable we analysts can be to our unanalyzed passions. And, of course, how vulnerable our patients can be to them too. If Silverberg, the very model of correctness, clear thinking, analytic precision, and integrity, could succumb, then certainly we lesser mortals could. One of the reasons for maintaining analytic distance is to attempt to prevent just this problem. However, it does not always succeed. My wife's first analyst was quite Freudian and he succumbed totally to her incredible seductiveness. She was so in love with him she used to sew a new dress, each one sexier than the last, for her sessions with him. And she would slip and call them "sexions." True, she was quite irresistible, the belle of the ball at all the analytic society's dances. To his credit, the analyst—now a very famous man and a teacher of mine while she was in treatment—had the integrity to tell her he was unable to treat her because of his feelings. Have I gotten into these kind of situations? Of course. I, too, would end my treatment when I became aware of my feelings interfering severely with my effectiveness. And of course they occurred much more frequently early in my career. Experience and self-knowledge help prevent them, or help the analyst deal with them in a manner that is not destructive either to the patient or to himself.

Needless to say, the analyst's reactions to the patient are regularly induced by the patient's unconscious, as are the patient's reactions to the analyst induced by his. But I am referring to instances when things get out of hand for the analyst, when he is obsessed in a positive or negative way by his patient. Currently I am treating a great beauty, a well-known actress. I embrace her in a fatherly way when the situation calls for it, but I never for a moment have an insistent erotic feeling toward her. Now, countertransferences are not necessarily erotic. They can be negative-angry, competitive, destructive, toward men as well as women. I have had competitive angry countertransference reactions to men who reminded me of my father. One such was to a very successful analyst more than ten years older than myself. At one point in treatment he pointed out that, when he was in trouble, I was wonderfully sympathetic; when he was strong and successful, however, I became competitive and even hostile to him. I had to acknowledge that he was right and I had been viewing him as my father. Insight into this process resulted in its diminution and I was able to continue to treat him.

Today, I am rarely caught up in a situation from which I cannot extricate myself rather quickly by analyzing the countertransference myself or with a colleague. But my point is that the classical analytic role—after all, Silverberg was the model of that in many ways—does not prevent these situations from occurring as it is claimed to do. I have come across quite a few patients who have had the most disastrous situations involving long-standing sexual experiences with their analysts, some of a classical persuasion, while still patients. I hardly say this is very common, but the feelings *not* expressed or acted on by the analyst can have almost as deleterious consequences to the treatment. I shall deal with this very important issue later on.

Voyage from Lesbos, about my homosexual patient who became heterosexual, proved very hard to publish. Perhaps in those days it was considered too prurient, though it was a very scientific case report. In any event, after literally thirteen rejections, I found a publisher. When my first book was accepted, I was ecstatic. It put me, as I saw it, into a different league—out of the ordinary run of the mill. It also started me on a whole sideline of writing: books, scientific papers, and even an occasional article for a popular magazine. This is my ninth book—I trust it won't be my last.

Once I had one book published, editors sought me out,

which was a pleasant change. No longer did I have to suffer through thirteen rejections. My second book was a simple *Handbook of Emotional Illness and Treatment*. A third, *The Analyst's Role*, completed about 1960, was written with two colleagues. In this book I began to explore the possibility of the analyst's changing the role he played, depending on the particular patient's needs. So with a patient who was afraid of dealing with a strong man, I advocated the analyst taking the stance of a strong man. With a patient who needed a warm, empathic figure, I advocated his being warm. The latter was really an anticipation of the role Heinz Kohut was later to suggest for the analyst in the treatment of certain patients. Our idea was that the analyst's neutrality and anonymity was not the most therapeutic attitude for all patients. Although I stopped far short of my present advocacy of authenticity, I was certainly moving away from a stereotypical analytic role with all patients. I like to say now that I disagree with everything I wrote in *The Analyst's Role*. In fact, I do. But that book was part of a genuine transition from the standard role to a more flexible one. Of course, nowadays the idea of any "role" for an analyst is repugnant to me. The only position I advocate is authenticity within the bounds of one's responsibility as a doctor and as an analyst. These latter bounds should be so ingrained as to rule out any grossly inappropriate response. Authenticity without undue conscious censorship should hopefully be the rule of the day.

In about 1960 I finally left Mama and Papa and acquired an office of my own. I had given up doing electric shock treatment for Dr. Impastato and even given up treating his psychotherapy patients for him. My fee with my first patient had been five dollars; now my fees had reached twenty-five dollars. I was able to dispense with most of my side jobs and devote myself mostly to private practice. An exception to this was my work as Director of Psychiatric Services at the Long Island Consultation Center. This sounded impressive, but certainly was not so at first. In

1953, four other professionals and myself rented a one-bed-room apartment in Forest Hills and started a clinic. The clinic has mushroomed incredibly. Today it treats over a thousand patients a week, trains almost thirty analytic therapists, puts out its own journal, has almost a hundred professionals on staff, and is a vital force in its community. My fee at the clinic was ten dollars an hour. I did psychiatric consultations, supervision, and teaching there; and that role has had a tremendous impact on my professional growth. There is no better way to clarify one's concepts and to learn to think clearly and precisely than to teach or supervise a bright, challenging student. Several of my students have opened clinics of their own; several have gone on to become teachers and writers, contributing to the field. In many ways I feel more paternal toward many of them than I do toward my own children. They are my "professional children." Since so much of my energy is invested in my work, I have often achieved a feeling of closeness to them, a pride in their achievements, and have welcomed their affection and respect. Some of them are good friends; many are acquaintances with strong bonds.

Along with this affiliation, which has continued for thirty years, I started doing free supervision for what was and continues to be a clinic to treat financially disadvantaged people, the Community Guidance Service. This organization also mushroomed and I did a great deal of supervising and teaching for it. Many of my patients have been former students of mine or their friends and relatives. One very effective way of advertising legitimately in my field is to supervise, teach, and write books or papers. For this reason, I have always had a plethora of patients. When people ask me, "How's business?" I usually truthfully answer, "Too good." I generally have a few more patients than I can comfortably handle. At present I have about fifty-five forty-five-minute patient or supervisory hours, and three groups. That is not exactly an easy schedule—but my grandfather trained me to work hard.

Along with these organizations, I became in about 1960 a member of the board of directors of the Society for the Scientific Study of Sex. When I joined the organization, it had a psychological approach to sexuality. In 1963 I had a book published called *Sexual Fulfillment and Self-Affirmation*. The central idea was that no one should ever have to read a book about sex, that one should be authentically and uniquely oneself in bed, with or without "kinks." The antithesis to this was, first, the Masters and Johnson, and then the Helen Singer Kaplan approaches, which teach people through sex therapy what to do by the numbers and tell them what they should feel. As the society moved closer and closer to a *1984* version of programmed sex, I got disenchanted with it and resigned.

At least three of my books in different areas have focused their attention on the issue of authenticity: the book on sex; one on child rearing called *Hold Them Very Close, Then Let Them Go;* and now this one. I believe a great damage has been done to our Selves—our subjective view of who we are—by programming our ways of being lovers, parents, or analysts. I believe this kind of dictation to people, which they appear only too eager to follow, destroys the essence of their experience and also the essence of their partner's. This is true whether the partner is a lover, a child, or a patient. So this is my third book in which the main argument advocates breaking away from previously prescribed paths.

7

Subjectivity

It is 1960. I have accomplished all that I set out to do, and then some. I have been married for ten years to a wife who is judged by my peers to be a most beautiful, charming, gracious, accomplished woman. I have two extraordinarily bright, attractive children—a boy, nine, and a girl, fourteen, to make the picture perfect. I have a lovely apartment in a fashionable suburb, Riverdale, and an office in the best part of town, 78th Street off Madison. My practice is flourishing, so that I almost always have a waiting list. I am the psychiatric head of one of the largest clinics in the country. I teach and supervise at three different analytic training institutes and have already begun to acquire a coterie of "groupies." I am well off financially, not only from my practice, but from the money I invested, which has quadrupled. I have been to Europe several times and to Central America, and spend part of each winter in the Caribbean. I am one of the first in my circle to have a European car; I am winning club tennis tournaments; I have had three books and several professional papers published. Even my Giants and Knicks are doing well. I am the envy of all my colleagues in my analytic society, most of whom covet my wife and show it in not too subtle ways. I am involved in a social whirl of dinner parties and dances, mostly with analytic colleagues. We usually spend our social time taking apart our former teachers and supervisors and others of our fraternity. There is a relatively pleasant, open competition between us that I can generally win in almost every department. To say, "I never had it so good," would be an understatement. My last analyst, Silverberg, was a good one and I feel practically no anxiety. So—how come I don't feel happy? Is this all there is? I look longingly at some of my patients, my colleagues' wives, my wife's friends. I look, but I don't touch. I have been monogamous for ten years. Since my wife looks and acts like a combination of Gina Lollabrigida and Sophia Loren and is Italian-Italian, fiery, and sexy to boot, this is relatively understandable. It is also a function of my having become very square, very caught up in the establishment of my subculture.

Analytically, I am still a relatively firm believer in Freudian theory, although a bit of a maverick when it comes to technique. I don't use the couch very much and I see my patients once or twice a week rather than more often. I am not rigid by comparison to my colleagues, but I *am* compared to former periods in my life. "Creeping meatballism" is gradually descending on me, like *The Invasion of the Body Snatchers*. And as in that movie, I am so taken over by my environment that I hardly notice the gradual loss of my Self. In the outside world people are beginning to talk about Zen Buddhism, Timothy Leary, and psychedelic drugs. The "beat generation" is beginning to appear. I think all of that stuff is some kind of craziness and cultism. Basically I remain within my professional, social, and sexual fortress, apparently quite impregnable at that point to any possibility of change.

Meanwhile at my clinic the seeds of subversion begin to be sown from a most unexpected quarter. I am the supervisor of the supervisors—the holy of holies, one step removed from God. The staff therapists work with the patients who come into the clinic but their work is monitored by an elite cadre of supervisors. In turn, the supervisors' work with their staff therapists is checked out by me. At thirty-seven I am already the person of last resort, the Supreme Court and the President. About ten supervisors work with me once a week for an hour or two. They present me their problems. This staff member is resistant to learning; that one is constantly coming on to his patients without even being aware of it—his supervisor calls him a "schlong-therapist"; another therapist fails to collect fees from his patients and lets them build up a balance as a way of ingratiating himself. I am Solomon dispensing answers and words of wisdom.

Gradually a trend develops in our meetings of supervisors. Several of the supervisors are in group therapy, some of them with an analyst of Zen-Buddhist persuasion. At first I think that they and their group therapist may be clinically psychotic. But slowly they begin to interact with one another as if they are in a therapy group. I have had only a brief twelve-session experience with group therapy in analytic school. This group told me I was cut off, defensive, and very difficult to approach in any intimate way so naturally I look upon group therapy with a great deal of suspicion. What could it really have to offer if the group I was in had so misperceived me—a lovable, open, available person?

Nevertheless, once this process of the supervisors interacting personally started, I somehow was unable to stop it. And, in effect, we quickly saw that most of the difficulties the supervisors were having with their supervisees stemmed from characterological resistances in the supervisors. For example, one was autocratic and put his supervisees in a defensive posture, a second was so falsely humble that he never gave any clear direction, and a third was so grandiose that he became hostile when he didn't get a standing ovation of appreciation. Once these resistances were attacked by the group, they began to soften, and supervision proceeded relatively unimpeded. But then we began to hit some snags in this process. Some of the supervisors felt that *my* characterological problems were keeping our group from proceeding as well as it could. Since the supervisors had dropped their immunity from scrutiny, perhaps I should drop my immunity as well. I am sure I believed this was more of their hippie egalitarian nonsense, but their argument was too persuasive and my inquiring mind was prodded.

So . . . they began to let me have it. And, of all the

strange things to happen, they said the same kind of things that my group in analytic school had said. They told me I was cut off, defensive, difficult to approach; they added that I was emotionally dead, rigid, had no clear core of Self they could identify, that I was like a robot that had been wound up before performing. This was not exactly welcome news. I kicked and squirmed and fought them off. But a group is a very powerful force. I often tell my groups today, "If one person says you're a horse, he's psychotic. If two people say you're a horse, they're prejudiced. But if three people tell you you're a horse, enter the next race at Santa Anita." Ten people told me I was a horse—I entered the next race at Santa Anita. My character defenses began to crumble. I began to loosen up; then I began to experience anxiety as my controls lost some of their force. And I started to do some reading in Zen Buddhism as my colleagues suggested.

Meanwhile back at the office, I had been seeing a lovely, bright, charming young actress. She and I had liked each other from our first session, which had started in a strange way. She had just seen Alain Resnais's *Hiroshima Mon Amour*. The male protagonist was a Japanese actor. The film had moved her considerably (as it did me when I saw it later) and she had "fallen in love" with the actor. Though I am not Japanese, I did at that time have a quite remarkable resemblance to the slim ascetic actor in the film (now I look more like a Sumo wrestler). In any event, for her it was "love at first sight" along with a real double take when she walked into my office after just having left the film.

I liked her very much too. Although I say this, I do not mean literally that there was any erotic element on either side. We were just very attracted to one another as people, but very much within the bounds of our professional relationship. At the time that the group was beginning to penetrate not only my armor but also my Western objective view of the world, this patient (let me call her Helen) and I were working extremely well analytically. She was progressing by leaps and bounds in her treatment. Previously, she had been in a very unsuccessful treatment with a classical analyst from the New York Psychoanalytic Institute. With me she had been dealing analytically with her primitive feelings of wanting to bite her mother's ungiving breast (a subject still relatively taboo at the New York Psychoanalytic Institute, which is mostly concerned with Oedipal issues). Suddenly she developed a lump in her breast. I cannot prove there was a relationship, but I have seen this occur on a few occasions. It certainly reinforced my strong impression of the psychological cause of physical symptoms. This patient had characteristically turned her anger against herself. Now that these primitive impulses reached consciousness, she had done it again. Instead of biting her mother's breast, she had bitten her own. The lump was examined and found to be malignant. She had to have a radical mastectomy.

Helen was quite cut off as a person. She was estranged from her husband, had a very poor relationship with her parents, and was an only child. She had no lover she was close to and no children. There were acquaintances but no really close female friends. As I perceived it—I think correctly—I was the only person she knew who could provide her with any comfort in this crisis. As happened to Dr. Kris with his patient Marilyn Monroe, I felt my heart go out to her; I believed she now needed me more as a real person than as an analyst. My supervisors' group had loosened my defenses. My reading of Suzuki, Alan Watts, and other Zen-Buddhist writers had encouraged my trusting my feelings rather than my intellect. I told Helen that I would suspend our professional relationship and be her friend and visit her daily at the hospital. She was very appreciative.

I began visiting her every morning before my practice and every evening after it. She had the mastectomy. Luckily, the malignancy had not spread to the nodes. She was nevertheless very upset and I was the only person who could calm her anxiety. She was so overwhelmed with anxiety and had such a bad relationship with her parents that I had to serve as a buffer and tactfully let them know she could not handle any contact with them.

Early one morning I awakened with a very strange sensation. I felt my heart opening up and going out toward Helen. For a period that lasted about thirty seconds, I saw the world in a way that was totally different from anything I had experienced at any previous time. I believe I was having a so-called mystical experience. Society exhibits a rather strange dichotomy in its attitude toward this. If a dead person has had mystical experiences, they sanctify him and revere him; if a living person claims to have had one, they say he is either a charlatan or a psychotic. The very word "mystical" conveys connotations of something odd, esoteric, supernatural, connected with witchcraft and black magic, something beyond human comprehension, something undefinable. For this reason, I do not like the word, but I think I am stuck with it because it has always been used to refer to a certain kind of experience, which at the same time has always been said to be beyond description and beyond definition.

Well, I don't think this type of situation is so odd or so completely beyond description or definition. First of all, let me say that when such an experience has been reported, from no matter what century and by a member of whatever faith or even no faith at all, there has been such a remarkable similarity in the description that it is clear that it is a part of human experience. Yet it must be said that it is an experience rather few people achieve. There is a striking similarity among the Samadhi experiences of the Hindus, the Satori experiences of the Zen Buddhists, the mystical experience of the Christian martyrs and of the Hassidic Jews, and also those reported by some other people not connected with a particular religion. Further, there is some similarity between these experiences and those achieved at times with the hallucinatory drugs, such as LSD. There is also almost always a very important aftermath of these moments. The person achieves a sense of enlightenment that often produces a marked change in his view of life and his subsequent way of living. The aftermath is usually characterized by an inner peace and acceptance of life and a marked diminution in compulsive, goal-directed behavior.

Let me then go on to describe the so-called indescribable. Since I have had such an experience, I think I can report it fairly lucidly, though perhaps some of the feeling tone and the sensation in the experience itself cannot be properly transmitted by words alone. I want to repeat some of the details of my background because I think they might be important in the total understanding of the experience. As I have said, I had been brought up in an extremely compulsive, conventional, goal-directed way. I was pushed to succeed from the time I was a small child. I was brought up almost from infancy to deny all my own pleasures, needs, and feelings, and to make myself into a machine that would produce a successful career. I was pushed to tell time, read, memorize poetry, and do arithmetic when I was four years old. I was also totally indoctrinated (or was it "brainwashed"?) with the view that to enjoy onself is the worst form of sinful self-indulgence, that work is the only valuable and permissible activity.

At this point in my life, this patient of mine, Helen, whom I had always especially admired and liked, had been struggling rather successfully with a deep masochistic problem. When she developed breast cancer, I found myself feeling very deeply for her, almost experiencing her anguish and pain. I also found myself mobilized to do whatever was in my power to help alleviate her suffering. The degree of involvement I had emotionally with her was one I had practically never, if ever, experienced toward another human being. My wall cracked and I could feel genuine emotions of concern, sympathy, caring, wanting to help—all feelings I had experienced before but never to this degree.

I found myself going to the hospital every morning before work and every evening after it. I was tremendously involved in helping to make the situation as tolerable as postion of myself with all its measures and divisions, I had come across a wholly new and different way of experiencing myself—subjectively.

I was reminded of an analogy when a friend of mine said she would like to go over into Switzerland from Italy. She wanted to see Swiss people and the Swiss land. I explained to her that the people were exactly the same on both sides of the border; they looked the same, spoke the same language, and had the same customs. Furthermore the land was about the same—mountains and lakes. The border was an artificial separation, created by man. There was really no difference between one side and the other. Similarly, boundaries of time, place, and person are artifically emphasized by us to the exclusion of the oneness and the basic connection between people, places, and things. In this subjective frame, time and place are relative and circular rather than linear. Objective, realistic definitions of things continue, but lose some of their previous degree of importance. We are so used to looking at things in an "objective" way, however, that we cannot see what is most important and most real—the connection of time, place, and person.

Notice that there is nothing magical or otherworldly or even ecstatic about this experience. It is simply an enlightenment, another dimension in seeing oneself. Of course, it is such a revolutionary one in personal terms that people have constructed religions based on it and have described it in religious terms, such as finding God, discovering one's soul, and so forth. And indeed the religious concept of the soul is very much akin to what one feels in this kind of experience. It is an awareness of a part of oneself that is indestructible— that existed before birth and continues to exist after death. Concepts of reincarnation are to my mind a rather crude primitive expression of the same idea. To me, it is not that one is reborn in another life as a cow or a flower; rather, there is a part of us that transcends time and place as well as person, and that will exist in some form forever.

I trust I do not begin to sound either religious or psychotic at this point. It is really a very simple concept, and not at all esoteric, very much like the concept of the indestructibility of matter in physics. And some of the other ideas of the continuum between time and space have also been approached by physics and the ideas of relativity. The objective scientific approach has, in fact, in its laborious fashion, come upon the same ideas that can be reached more immediately subjectively and intuitively. Of course, the problem is that few people are ever able to use this part of themselves because the world around them suppresses it, systematically eroding it through upbringing and education.

All I am trying to show by a description of my own so-called mystical experience is that there is nothing really mystifying about it; it is simply a view of oneself and of the world through another eye which we all have but seldom use. As a matter of fact, the third eye is a symbol that is used in the Hindu religion to indicate the possibility we have of seeing ourselves in a way that is different and enlightening.

Now what happens to a person after he or she has such an experience? Usually, some very important things, which are relatively unexplainable in terms of our ordinary systems of psychology and psychoanalysis. How do we explain the conversion at the revival meeting of the thief into the solid citizen? How do we explain the "cure" of the chronic alcoholic after a so-called psychedelic LSD experience?

The point is that after we have gotten even a brief glimpse of ourselves in this perspective—and my experience lasted only a few seconds—we can no longer look at the world in the same way. Concern over survival, the achievement of socially accepted goals, money, success in work or sex or society, becomes relatively less important. Viewed from the perspective of a timeless, spaceless infinity, whether one's stock goes up or down, or whether one's girlfriend rejects or accepts one, just does not seem *that* crucial. Of course, we would still rather win than lose, succeed than fail, be loved rather than rejected. But all of these things become tangential from this new perspective. They do not touch the real central core of the Self or the Self-system. To be vulgar, they become the gravy rather than the meat and potatoes; so, whether we get a little more gravy today or a little less does not matter so much. Whether what we do is applauded or condemned is also much less important. What occurs after a mystical experience is a tremendous increase in what Freud called primary narcissism or healthy self-love. It is a core of caring for the Self and believing in its indestructibility, so that events of the external world have less effect on this basic constant in the equilibrium. As I write these things, I keep thinking how so many of these same ideas have been expressed, often with great beauty, in the writings of various religions. The only problem is that almost all religions are shored up with structure and dogma, so that their very nature militates against their members achieving the goals the founders embraced.

I want to clarify the difference between primary and secondary narcissism here and to show how it fits into my concept of subjectivity. Primary narcissism is this healthy self-love, this focus on subjectivity, this realization that *I* am more important to me than anyone else or anything else that exists, that *I* am the center of my universe, and that I can love myself, trust my intuition and feelings to do what is best for me no matter what the outside world or the non-Self says I should or shouldn't do. This is the feeling whose lack is at the base of all mental, emotional, and psychological or psychiatric problems. Call it what you will—a defective ego, a lack of self-esteem, trouble in the Self-system, a confused idealized image, or whatever—it is at the basis of all human mental suffering. Secondary narcissism is what we see as a reparative attempt when there is a basic lack of primary narcissism. It is an unsuccessful attempt to replace this essential lack by an exaggerated focus of attention on one's body or mind. It is characterized by marked ego-centricity and a constant or compulsive attempt to reach the Self. Primary narcissism is quite the opposite. The person *has* himself, so he does not jealously have to guard against losing himself through constant preoccupation with Self. He can, once having himself, "lose" himself in whatever he is involved with; he does not need to maintain a self-consciousness. This self-consciousness is to keep him from losing himself (losing his Self, that is). "Losing" oneself means being so sure of one's hold on one's Self through subjective Self-love that one can throw oneself—surrender totally—into whatever one is doing at the moment without any consciousness of Self. Wouldn't it be marvelous if one could restore one's primary narcissism in a direct way rather than painfully and laboriously trying to repair some of the holes that appear as a result of a basic leak in it? This is what I think psychoanalysis has been doing up until now. It has never dealt with the basic problem of subjectivity, because—with the possible exception of Jung—all of its adherents have been "unenlightened."

Perhaps a unique contribution I can make is that I have gone through all of the traditional discipline of becoming an analyst and practicing analysis, and have also had the rather unique experience of mysticism or heightened subjectivity or whatever one may want to call it. I do not want to go on describing the mystical experience at greater length because this has been done many times before and certainly more beautifully and poetically than I could ever manage (though rarely without elements of magic, religion, or the supernatural connected with it). Also I am sure there are many analysts who are sharper psychoanalytic theoreticians than I. However, I do feel I might have something rather unique to offer in my attempt to combine these two points of view, synthesize them, and perhaps help to come up with an approach that has more promise than the one-dimensional, so-called objective, realistic, "scientific" analytic viewpoint.

What happens to one after such a mystical experience? What did the so-called mystical experience do for me? First of all, though it lasted for just a short time, I found I could revive it through meditation and I have always been able to maintain, granted to varying degrees, the perspective and the enlightenment achieved in it. By meditation, incidentally, I don't mean thinking about it; rather, meditation is a process of "mind-clearing." One clears one's mind of all thought and all connections with the outside. And from this one achieves a heightened sense of one's Self. I do not want to give the idea that I go into such meditations or trances daily. Actually, I think I have done it four times in the past year. I now find little need to reinforce my perspective either through meditation or even through reading in this field, because what happens after a mystical experience is that one has a much more solid core of healthy Self-interest and Self-belief. I now am free to do much less planning and structuring of my life, and am more apt to take things as they come. The good things give me joy but not ecstasy. The bad things upset me for a while but they depress me seriously less frequently than they used to do.

I must say that immediately after the mystical experience, I did have a period of elation and great joy, freedom and personal expansiveness. This was followed by a period of quite great anxiety and at times quite severe depression, while I grappled with the attempt to base my security in myself and gradually let go of my outside props. The process of doing this can be quite frightening and distressing. Luckily I was able to get through it without giving up or retreating to my previous position.

How do I feel today, after all this time? I feel anxious or depressed much less frequently. Sometimes I can look at life as the unfolding of an interesting adventure. I try to think less about past or future, and to be involved in whatever I am doing at the moment. I can involve myself more deeply with people than ever before. I follow my intuition and I trust it both professionally and otherwise; it gets me farther than my logical thinking does, though I can still use my logical thinking when my intuition fails me. I lead a less structured life: I try to do what I want to do, what I *feel* like doing, whether it is conventional or not. I have less investment in people's approval or disapproval of me. Then why am I writing this book? Because I have something that *I* want to express. It is *my* creative thinking. I would prefer people to applaud it, but I will not be devastated if they don't. I care much less for possession of things or money, or for that matter, of people. I have the feeling that I'll be around and I want to see what's coming up next.

It is like choosing a movie to go to. One does not always choose comedies or movies with happy endings; one goes to adventure stories, tragedies, thrillers, and so on. I similarly have the conviction that life will not always be peaceful or happy, but I feel, whatever comes up, it will be interesting to experience. Meanwhile, I try to throw myself into what I'm doing, whether it's writing or practicing or playing tennis. I trust myself to know that I'll go after what my mind and body tell me that I want—at least much of the time. It's only when I don't that I feel really disappointed with myself. To quote the Zen philosophy about the meaning of life: "When you're hungry, you eat; when you're tired, you sleep." That is really all this is about—to follow your own impulses and intuitions and not to box yourself into any structure that limits your freedom.

This "satori" experience was the culmination of what would today be called my midlife crisis, and it affected me deeply. I had discovered what was missing in my "perfect" life—a mystical, spiritual thread. I was pushed by inner forces to go through a period of severe tension and anxiety as I began to loosen my structures. My way of looking at the world and at my patients had to change. I did not discard the old Freudian theories, but I became less rigid in their application.

The early sixties was a very dynamic period; radical change was the order of the day in science, in art, in music, and in philosophy. A major trend throughout the creative world was in the direction of the Eastern subjective philosophical approaches and away from the Western objective ones. Subjectivism was beginning to creep into psycho-

sible for her. At this point, one morning at about 4 or 5 A.M. I awoke from sleep with a tremendous feeling of concern for her. I felt as if my heart were just bursting out of my body and opening up and going out toward her. Suddenly I experienced a very cool, peaceful feeling—*not* an exalted or ecstatic one. At first I felt the connection between myself and her, then the connection between myself and all other people. After this breaking through of the separation between people, I experienced the same feeling of the lack of separations in time and place as well as between persons. It seemed as if yesterday, today, and tomorrow were all one, and as if geographical as well as temporal divisions were meaningless. In essence, it was a way of looking at the world without the usual separations in time, place, and person. My experience emphasized the oneness and the connection between things rather than the separations between them. Instead of the space between me and the chair being paramount, the connection between me and the chair was, and the space was also part of the *connection* between us rather than the separation of us. With respect to time, I felt as if I could be in the fifteenth century or perhaps could tell what would happen tomorrow. Time, space, and person all became a rounded, inclusive continuum rather than a series of separated, unconnected objects.

Along with this feeling of timelessness, spacelessness, and personlessness also came a feeling of my own immortality and indestructibility. Let me explain this. If I was a part of all things, all people, all time, and all space, my concern about my own survival and the small problems that seemed so threatening and important in everyday life diminished considerably. I had experienced myself in a way that was totally different from anything I had felt before. What it amounts to is that I was now focused in a very concentrated way on my own Self and my own subjectivity. The way the world had always been presented to me, the picture of so-called external objective reality, still existed, but it was of diminished importance to me. By losing my external defini-

analysis, too, but at a rather slow rate. The vast majority of psychoanalysts were not only not allowing their own views to be influenced by the changes around them but were shoring up their old positions more zealously, afraid that if they caught up with the rest of the creative frontier, they would not be able to use any of their older thinking, training, and experience. There was a strong battle against subjectivism and "irrationality" in psychoanalysis. I learned, however, that form, structure, and objective reality are not the only ways of approaching an understanding of man. Existentialism, Zen Buddhism, and mysticism give another approach from an entirely new frame of reference, one that does not dispute the validity of the objective scientific frame of reference but adds another dimension to our thinking. For an analyst, it is helpful to examine every new approach in hopes of its leading to a broader understanding of man that might, in turn, give us clues to new theories and "techniques" of helping a person who is troubled.

Perhaps before going into the application of subjectivism to psychoanalytic theory and practice, I should define more clearly exactly what I mean by subjective versus objective. Let us go back to the beginning of life to arrive at an understanding of this. When a child is born, he has a mass of feelings and responses within himself—when he is cold, he has a certain kind of unpleasant feeling; when he is hungry, he has another kind of feeling; when a person treats him well, he feels good and comfortable; and when he is mistreated, he has a perception of this too. He knows his own feelings, but he is also helpless and dependent. Then people come around and they put labels and names on what occurs around him and even on what he feels. He may feel hungry, but his mother puts a blanket on him instead of feeding him. He becomes confused: his own perceptions do not agree with the perceptions of those around him. However, his security lies in maintaining his dependency on those around him. In order to do this, he gradually begins to put aside his own feelings and his own knowledge and perceptions, and to live by what others tell him is there, what others perceive.

When the perceptions of the others around him do not differ too much from his own inner ones, then he is in good shape and will grow up fairly well. However, when the outside perceptions are quite consistently in disagreement with his own, he will gradually begin to give up more and more of himself in order to gain the security and stability of the agreement and approval of those around him. What feels like hate to him, his mother calls love. He begins to think of it as love too, but he can only do this by denying a part of himself in the process. If there is too much disparity between his real Self and the outside, he will grow up with very little contact with the real feeling part of himself at all. His perceptions will be replaced by other people's labels of what he is supposed to perceive, and he will believe these labels. His feelings will also be dictated from outside forces rather than inside ones. Pretty soon his only concept of himself will be dictated from the outside and he will have lost much of his contact with his own wishes. We see many patients who really have little idea who they are, what they feel, or what they want. All of us are like this to some degree, but some of us more so than others.

The objective focus on external reality that occurs in the usual analytic procedures is unable to do much to reverse this process. Granted that, in a way, the lifting of repression and the process of making conscious what has been unconscious is a partial attempt at more contact with the inner Self. On the other hand, the structure of the analytic situation in the classical sense is so tight and so formal and the analyst himself so objective that this militates against a true focus on subjectivity in the patient. The analyst is a model as well as a doctor. How can the patient dare risk leaving the security of the objective, to be thrown back to his own primitive primary feelings and to the original position of aloneness without anyone on whom to depend, if the analyst meanwhile is sticking to the strictest possible structure regarding time, money, office, relationship; stressing, in fact, impersonality and complete objectivity? What the patient needs is to reestablish his own belief and trust in the correctness of his own subjective perceptions and feelings. It is a dangerous though rewarding leap from the security of the known. But he needs an analyst who already has taken the major leap for himself and who is continuing to take these leaps. The patient must have a guide for his perilous journey.

The position of Freud and almost all of his followers with the exception of Jung was to accept the objective realistic philosophical position. This leads to seeing the world around us as the important reality, and our adaptation to it or adjustment to it as the most important aspect of growing and maturing as a person. The problem, stated or unstated, then becomes how to get the patient to adapt in a better way to his environment.

But suppose we begin to question the importance of the whole objective position. Suppose we think that what is outside of ourselves is essentially not all-important. Suppose we think that each one of us is the center of the universe and can make the world through our minds essentially into whatever we want it to be, regardless of what is objectively out there. In schizophrenia, a person does this by shutting out or distorting external reality. But without being schizophrenic we can have a major role in shaping what for us is out there in terms of being selectively attentive or inattentive to different aspects of our experience. The optimist looks through rose-colored glasses while the pessimist's glasses have a somewhat darker tinge. So we can work on the part of ourselves that can shape our experience into essentially what we would like it to be. By getting to our own subjective Selves, in touch with our being, our feelings, our likes and dislikes, we have the freedom to try to view the world in our own image and to make it what we want it to be. Then suddenly, instead of being little cogs in a big wheel that we have to adjust to, we become the wheel itself.

There is no longer a duality between the subjective and the objective, and all our adaptational struggles disappear, having been neatly transcended by our point of view.

To use more Freudian terms, the objective point of view parallels the child's position in relationship to the parents. The person is the small insignificant one in relationship to the large world; he is the slave and not the master. In this position he will feel helpless, dependent, and restricted—the pre-Oedipal positions—and will have the attendant rage when he is deprived or restricted. In the subjective position, *he* is the master and the world around him is the slave. This is closer to the mature position, but it is a great deal more than that. Since the person is essentially creating his own world, he does not feel dependent, restricted, or helpless. It is true that he is not really omnipotent and some of what he experiences will be sadness, disappointment, and frustration. But since he feels he is essentially the master, he could—if he wished to—shut these out. However, the important thing in life is not constant joy but constant experiencing. In this frame of reference, tragedy is a great deal easier to bear.

Not long after I had my experience with the mystical, my life changed radically. I was to leave my wife, I broke off relationships with many of my colleagues; I left my analytic society, and became more of a searcher and a maverick. I became involved with a woman who was very mystical and spiritual, and had social intercourse with her friends who were mainly in the arts. I also began to experience a great deal of anxiety and needed my supervisors' group for support. The king had really toppled from his throne. I became even more questioning than before of Freudian analytic dogma, and began to understand my patients from a more subjective point of view. I attended some lectures by Timothy Leary, the Harvard psychology professor who supported the use of LSD, and some of his followers. Luckily for me, I believe, I was not that much taken with him and did not get into the frame of taking psychedelic drugs as some of my colleagues did. (I once did volunteer to take LSD as part of a research study at a hospital, but the study was called off.)

For many people at that time and subsequently it was very tempting to use drugs as a way to try to experience new perspectives on life. I cannot say I have ever met a person who developed any lasting insight or enlightenment from taking hallucinogenic drugs. On the other hand I think that my thirty-second brush with "satori" did cause a profound shift in the way I experienced the world. I don't think I have ever been the same since that thirty-second experience. This is what others who have had similar experiences consistently report. I think the experience helped make me flexible and open to other analytic ideas as well as to people. By opening up a new way of seeing the world that was totally unknown to me, I could never again be certain of any position I took or hold to it rigidly. It also helped me to move toward a more subjective focus in therapy, to trust my own free associations when I am with a patient, and to use *these* rather than objective formulas as the basis of my responses to patients. If, while a patient is speaking, I have a thought or fantasy, I often communicate it to him or her even if it seems irrelevant. This is the antithesis of an objective Freudian communication.

To give an example, once a patient was talking about her inability to capitalize on her talents. I began to think of the death of my sister when I was seven and she was five. I communicated my thought processes to the patient and we wondered about the connection. Of course! The patient's sister had died when the patient was seven and her sister was two. But what had this to do with her inability to maximize her talents? After a few associations of mine and hers, we saw that a compulsive need to make reparations over guilt about her sister's death had inhibited her effective aggression just as my own aggression once had been similarly inhibited. The therapeutic process had been an exciting one of mutual enlightenment, not a dull uncreative one of my making an intellectual interpretation about her.

This example is not such a rare instance. When the analyst participates in the process—not as Sullivan suggested as a "participant observer," but as an equal, subjective participant using *his* unconscious process—then analysis becomes an activity of mutual creation. It is similar to two artists standing side by side, each painting his own picture, who are connected by their mutual commitment to creativity but do not encroach on one another's autonomy. Instead of a master–pupil dependency, the situation is more analogous to parallel play in children. This environment fosters autonomy rather than the pathological dependency that is automatically set up in the classical analytic relationship, where the analyst is the objective, "well," omniscient one and the patient the "sick," unknowing one. The classical relationship fosters the idea, "Turn yourself over to me. I am your superior. I know best." My subjective egalitarian relationship disputes the myth that there is "someone up there watching over you." It shows that the analyst is as subject to his history and his unconscious as is the patient. It tries to dispel the idea that a Self can be acquired by "finding another person who knows the answers." "Someday my prince will come" is a myth that seduces us to give up our Selves and pin our hopes on salvation by Another. My motto is better expressed in Lily Tomlin's line: "Remember, we are all in this alone." But that is not a cynical statement. We can have parallel play with others who can share our aloneness.

In my office, once a climate has been established in which the patient feels the analyst's intense empathic connection to him, the analyst and the patient can share this aloneness. They both follow their own creative process, which stems from their unconscious. However, the analyst's is reactive to the patient's verbal and nonverbal productions—not simply his own psyche. Their connection then is not one of symbiosis or parasitism, but one of two autonomous Selves doing their own thing at the same time and in the same place, given the analyst's essential empathic focus on the patient. This hardly happens in every session, but it happens often enough. The ideal session is one in which both patient and therapist allow themselves to be open and vulnerable to each other, so that both achieve not only an enlightenment and a connection to their unconscious creative processes but also the experience of doing this *à deux,* with another person present, participating but neither intruding nor carrying nor engulfing.

Classical psychoanalysis pretends to be analysis *à un.* The patient and his unconscious is the only one in the room. The analyst is merely a "blank screen." Even if this were true, it would leave out the excitement of parallel play; classical analysis is certainly *not* exciting, to the degree that the analyst is often fighting sleep. What really goes on is that the analyst is perceived as the all-knowing parent. In my opinion, many people who have been through classical analysis—including the analysts—come out of it as I came out of my three classical analyses. They are conforming children who have lost their uniqueness and creativity. That might very well have been my fate, and the fate of my patients, had I not had a supervisors' group and an introduction to Zen Buddhism, and the courage to face my overwhelming terror at giving up the security of conformity. Such terror at that point in life is not pathological but an inevitable concomitant of the rite of passage from being conforming to being creative, from being bound to being free.

I am certainly not implying that setting up a climate in the analytic situation that promotes freedom will bring about a "satori" experience in a patient. Actually, this has happened only once in my practice. However, I believe that the analyst's having this point of view promotes actualization and healthy emotional separation. I also believe that the analyst's having a mystical orientation as a base can help both analyst and patient to keep even major tragedies in the perspective of a broader view of the world and the universe. It can foster a view that life goes on despite periods of misfortune. It can also help us view misfortune from the position of the "absurdity" and "meaninglessness" of any one specific incident or individual in the broader picture of the whole. From this perspective, one can have a sense of humor about the most devastating blows. I believe in and use a great deal of humor in my therapy. This is not mutually exclusive of a caring, empathic response to a patient's pain. Instead, it sets up a universal frame-work in which specific pain can be tolerated and dealt with more comfortably.

Of course, I am not trying to say that classical analysis necessarily prevents the process of creativity and freedom. I just feel that all too frequently it does not promote it. An analyst must have had the courage to go through a kind of death and resurrection or he will never allow his patient to risk this dangerous passage. The idea of "counterresistance" is based on the theory that an analyst will not allow, will turn a deaf ear to the patient's attempt to venture into any arena that is too frightening for the analyst; he will unconsciously be selectively inattentive to material that he has not worked through from his own unconscious. This concept of counterresistance is not particularly popular with classical analysts, but I feel it is of great importance, and I use the concept a great deal in supervision. But patients who are interested in going through a "rite of passage" must be very careful in selecting an analyst. They not only have to check on his or her credentials; even more important, they must find out what kind of person he or she is, how open, how courageous, how undefended. Choosing an analyst is perhaps even more crucial than choosing a mate. The analytic process opens very tender areas that either can be nurtured sensitively or squashed without the analyst's conscious choice to do so. Beware of gurus who "know the world" and will subtly impose it on you. Watch out for the "Invasion of the Body Snatchers." The Surgeon-General says that analysis can be injurious to your Self.

8

My Venture into Group Therapy

With this great cataclysm in my life and the "destruction" of my past, I now had to find a new path for resurrection. One of the important professional impacts of my "transformation" was the awakening of an interest in group therapy. After all, it was the group at the Long Island Consultation Center that had cracked through my rigid character armor and sprung me loose. I realized that this kind of metamorphosis could never have occurred to me as a result of individual analysis alone. The power of numbers, for one thing, is tremendous. I had never been very much interested in group therapy, in which, as most readers are probably aware, a group of about eight people meet with a therapist, usually for an hour and a half weekly. I had read some of the standard books on it and not been much impressed.

The fashionable way of conducting a group at the time was characterized by Samuel Slavson and Alexander Wolf. Wolf, as a matter of fact, was a member of my analytic society and the leader of the group I had been in during my analytic school days. He was a very debonair man, who maintained the position of a somewhat amused observer of the scene from above—"What fools these mortals be." I did not know Slavson personally, but his book advocated quite a detached position for the analyst. What both Slavson and Wolf were doing, and what most group therapists still do, amounts to individual analysis in a group. After all, group therapy had been started during World War II as an expedient. There were not enough psychiatrists to go around for each patient individually, so perforce soldiers were seen in groups. One of the group therapists whose work I admire but only came to understand in the late seventies is an Englishman, Wilfred Bion, who was exposed to groups exactly in this way when he was in the Army. With the exception of Bion, who dealt with groups as entities in themselves rather than a collection of individuals, the group therapy movement, in my opinion, had always had individual analysis as a basic model. For this reason, I have never associated myself with any of the established group therapy associations.

I had stumbled into my model for group therapy fortuitously. My group at the Center had been one in which I was the nominal leader, but I was basically incapable of leading since I knew less about group therapy than most of the people in my group. Not only did *I* make tremendous changes but almost everyone else in the group went through important if not quite such dramatic changes. I do not know if I conceptualized it consciously then, but later I hit on the idea that it is the very fact of having a leader who cannot and does not lead that forces people to give up their wish to find security through dependency. This in turn forces them to take responsibility for themselves and to maximize whatever assets they possess in order to survive in the best way possible. I am sure that at that point I had not totally thought this through. In retrospect, I can also see the influence of my readings in Zen and the influence of the period. My role was not dissimilar to that of the Zen master. When the student asks him to explain the meaning of life, the master hits him over the head with a stick. Much of Zen theory has to do with letting go of attachments to people, to possessions, to rules of behavior, to concepts. It is the very search for meaning and structure, for leaders who "Know the answer," that creates the difficulties in our life. Of course, existential philosophers picked up on this theme: there is no past and no future; the only moment to be in is the present. The only meaning is Being.

I think that my role in my original group, which in a sense occurred by accident, led me to think about conducting my own groups in this way. As far as I know, my way of doing group therapy is unique. I have called it a "leaderless" group, but it differs from other leaderless groups, such as peer groups in which there in fact is no leader. I am the leader. I get paid. I am the professional. At the same time I acknowledge that I am neither intellectually nor emotionally superior to the members. True, I have professional expertise. But unlike a Zen master, who has transcended worldly problems, I am often as lost, helpless, vulnerable, and despairing as any of my patients. I don't have any more of "the Truth" than they. I struggle daily and have to deal with all of my own emotional foibles. I have to be open with my patients about who I am, what my struggles are, what my pain is. They must know as much about me as I know about them; they must rescue me when I am drowning, just as the group at the Center did. The Zen master knows there are no answers. I demonstrated that I did not have the answers and so destroyed their illusions that I or someone else might have such answers.

First of all, it is not surprising that other analysts and group therapists would not and could not happily embrace this position. They may be more defensive about their own neurosis, or too self-protective to allow this amount of exposure of self. I am really *not* concerned about hiding myself, as I used to be. When I first started conducting groups in this way, I was afraid all my patients would leave me if they found out I had been divorced. I am now at a point in a process that has gone on for more than twenty years. Each revelation of a particular new neurotic problem of mine, such as my lack of a close relationship to my children, my difficulties in intimate relationships, my tendency toward depression, was accompanied by tremendous anxiety on my part. Would I be accepted if I did not fit into the group's norm? Each time I took the risk of being my own idiosyncratic Self, I discovered to my amazement that nothing world-shaking occurred. Many of my patients did and still do disapprove of my attitudes and behavior in many areas;

often their criticisms are well founded. But my survival in the group or in the world (for the group is, among other things, a microcosm) is not really conditional upon their acceptance. I suppose I may have lost a patient here or there because of their disapproval of me, but I would be hard put to name a specific instance. And my clientele has included strict Orthodox Jews, extremely conforming Catholics, left-wing political activists, Hollywood and socialite people who were "into" glamour—a wide variety. If you have the courage to be yourself, you may be shunned, but more often people will admire your courage unless you are totally outrageous. Of course, my taking these risks with them was a model for my patients to try to drop those parts of themselves that were largely false and in the service of conformity rather than genuine expressions of Self.

Paradoxically, the group used as a way of effecting change the very process it was attempting to defeat: conformity to the environment. The group norm became autonomous individuality. Any verbalization or behavior that opposed this, including pleasing me, was attacked. So through the old Pavlovian method of reward and punishment (autonomy was rewarded and conformity was punished), people were forced to risk showing more of their real Selves and dropping parts of their false Selves. This idea of a real and false Self was one that was highlighted by the English analyst Donald W. Winnicott, who worked a good deal with children. From the time we are born, we are subjected to conditioning in the old Pavlovian way. Certain behaviors are rewarded and others are punished. We quickly learn that we cannot be accepted for being who we are; yet our very life in infancy seems to us to depend on this acceptance. So we begin to hide our feelings and to conform to these outside norms. We develop a false Self, which was termed by Jung a "persona." If our environment has been reasonably permissive and encouraging of our being individual and "special," we will sacrifice some, but not an enormous amount, of our true Selves. But if, as is the case of too many of us, our environment has been rigid in insisting on conformity, we may lose touch in a major way with who we are. We may become conforming robots who have learned survival but not being.

Many of my patients—all very well functioning—had lost touch with their essence. This is the precise issue that got me so disenchanted with the sex therapists and their tendency to program "normal" sexual activity. Since sexual knowledge and behavior were suppressed, that was one area at least in which we did not have a pattern to which to conform. We were told what *not* to do, so many of us did very little or expressed only a small part of our sexual potential. But at least we were not told what to do. Now we have atlases with photos of all the positions and permutations and combinations. So many people who today mechanically and behaviorally do all the "right" things in bed, do them because they are following a formula rather than expressing their own idiosyncratic Selves.

The reason we lose our real Selves and develop facades is because we need to conform in order to be nurtured and protected by our parents as infants—our lives literally depend on it. Then, once this way of relating has become an established pattern, we are conditioned to continue it. Over and over we keep coming back to Pavlov. His ideas on conditioning through reward and punishment are so simple, yet so profound. A good case could be made for psychoanalysis being a very complicated, sophisticated deconditioning process. However, I feel many analysts subtly reinforce conformity by presenting themselves as models of proper adaptations. Certainly this theory of deconditioning could be applied very cogently to the process in my own groups. The patients are put in a situation with a parental surrogate: they look to him for the answers on how to feel and how to behave. He refuses to give them the answers, but so do most silent analysts. The difference between me and them is that they continue to maintain, through their silence, the illusion that they have the answers. The patient then waits around to find little clues as to what behavior and feelings are rewarded by the analyst. And of course he finds them, through tones of voice, selective attentions or inattentions, the analyst's mode of dress, place of office, general behavior. So the patient usually assumes that the analyst is the model of conformity. In fact, he is often correct. There have of course been many orthodox analysts whose private lives were quite outrageous but who were very careful to present a proper conforming facade to the patients. I remember even my old nonconforming training analyst commenting to me on how embarrassed he was when a "fancy lady" patient of his saw him walking along the street eating an ice-cream cone, not acting like a proper gentleman.

So what happens is that most patients who are in classical analysis for a long time become very dead, conforming people. I certainly did. My years with my first analyst, my training analyst, and then Silverberg all reinforced my false Self and hid my true Self. I had to hide the evil parts of myself and present an acceptable facade. Perhaps my training analyst may even have been a bit of fresh air—at least in terms of not presenting this model of conformity. Now I pride myself upon not presenting this front. I rarely wear a jacket and tie—only when there is a special occasion that must be attended after my workday. My office is hardly the model of anonymity. Strangely, it is not unlike Freud's office. It is filled with pieces of primitive art (I am a collector) and other expressions of my Self. My books, including autobiographical ones, are at my patients' disposal. I do not want to hide who I am and thus, by example, encourage them to hide who they are; I do not want them to come to me because I am such a model of "mental health" and conformity to society. What is "mental health"? Is it the ability to adapt to society? Well, in truth, adapting is one of the functions of the ego. Without it, we would not be able to survive. Darwin certainly pointed out in terms of species survival that ability to adapt to the environment was central. I feel that one must have the *ability* to adapt to the environment. For instance, I have to pay my taxes and get to my appointments on time. But I feel this has to be a choice, an option, not something that occurs outside of one's awareness like a chameleon's change of colors.

Mental health seems to me to be a function of the ability to be one's own unique Self as much as is possible. This does not preclude one's ability to adapt when survival of one sort or another depends on it. For instance, I can behave myself and fit in when I must, but I find more and more situations in life in which I truly have a choice in this matter. To give some examples, I used to feel that I had to have dinner with friends or colleagues—that it was important to have a social life, that I had to have a relationship with my parents and children, that I had to attend certain psychoanalytic meetings. Now I find that I consult my feelings in these matters. If I feel that situations are unrewarding for me and that I just go through the motions in them, I avoid them. There are very few people with whom I truly enjoy spending time so *my* group of friends is very limited. I know I enjoy watching sports on TV, so I do it to my heart's content. My life is very different from what it was before my "transformation." Then, my leisure time was spent in rounds of dinner parties with analytic colleagues; these were the height of dullness and only bearable through the use of alcohol. In the same way, I encourage my patients to examine what parts of their lives are truly chosen out of option rather than conformity to an established structure. For many people this is quite a revolutionary attitude.

I want to clarify some issues around this point of adaptation. First of all, I do not think my method of conducting groups can be used for all kinds of patients. I would hardly apply it to a group of convicts in prison or a group of schizophrenics. In fact, I do not even apply it to all the patients I have in individual analysis. There are some patients who for whatever reasons—and I am not expressing a pejorative opinion about them—are so entrenched in their subculture (perhaps even happily so) that this kind of group would be upsetting without being therapeutic for them. It would stir feelings of change in them that they would not have a real desire to actualize, such as leaving their job or their wife. The only people I place in my groups are well-functioning neurotic patients who have a strong will to actualize themselves rather than just relieve their symptoms. When I have put more disturbed people into a group of mine, it has been bad both for them and for the group. Also, as much as I attempt to be honest, authentic, and self-revealing, I never abdicate my responsibility as a doctor. I set up the structure of the group in terms of time, payment, and choice of new additions. If a group gets bogged down—if there is a group resistance because of unwillingness to face some issues—then it is my responsibility to get them "off the dime." I will protect someone who has become the group "scapegoat" and is no longer able to defend himself. Doesn't that oppose the idea that there is no one who is there to take care of you? Perhaps. The system is not perfect. I cannot be the doctor and also a totally self-interested person simultaneously at times. In fact, though, with the patient population I have described, this situation practically never occurs. Other group members will come to the rescue of their own accord. No one I put in a group will allow himself to become *that* much of a masochistic victim. I may come to the rescue because of my humanity—not because of my medical responsibility.

I have to step in very rarely. For instance, I have practically never stepped in as a doctor when either sex or physical violence has taken place either within the group or outside it among members. I am very clear that my role is *not* to be a policeman or an authority. The only rule I have in group is confidentiality; this, of course, applies to me, but also to every member. Many groups have very firm rules about not allowing violence in the group, not allowing communication between members (even in the waiting room), not allowing sex between group members. For certain kinds of groups with more disturbed patients, with the objective of support rather than change, these rules may make eminent sense. They would clearly be counterproductive for my groups and my objectives. If what I wish a patient to attempt to achieve is autonomy, I can scarcely set myself up as a judge or a policeman. The people I take into my groups are well-functioning, responsible adults. If their behavior should violate any of the laws of the state, they—not I—would be responsible.

In fact, my patients practically never have and never will violate any legal rule. When there have been outbursts of violence—perhaps five times in over twenty years—they have been quite contained by the patients' own structure. Rarely have other group members needed to intervene. I do not recall ever intervening myself. There have certainly been sexual involvements between members of my groups. Since the group is basically a microcosm, as sexual mores changed over twenty years, sexual involvements increased. When I started doing group therapy, being single and not being a virgin was shameful; nowadays, being a virgin is shameful. Still, I recall no instances of any deleterious consequences of any of these involvements, nor have they been numerous.

I am a person, too, and if I am going to be authentic in the group, I have to be honest about my feelings, as well. I have sexual feelings about some women in my groups and I express them. It does not constitute a big problem either for them or for me. I certainly do not allow myself to express my feelings other than verbally. Sexual involvements between analysts and patients can be and often are disastrous for both of them, but especially for the patient because of the obvious inequality in the relationship. I have seen quite a few of the disastrous results of such relationships. As to anger, I show it when I feel it, which is not very often. If this should get out of hand—which has never to this point happened—other group members would move in to curb me.

When I am despondent over some professional, financial, or interpersonal problem, I express my feelings about it to the group and eventually they are usually sympathetic and supportive. However, at first when the group sees that I am human and fallible, they want no part of that. I get attacked for not being the person they can idealize and look to for "the answers" and for a model of mental health.

At this juncture I would like to include a letter from one of my patients received while I was away on vacation, as well as my response to it.

Dear Dick,

I thought that if you would send me a post card from Sweden, that it would at least have a picture of a good looking Swedish girl on the front. Lo to my surprise, a fuggin can of Campbell's Soup. . . . That's not the kind of tomato I had in mind!!! [As a joke, I had sent him a Pop Art card.] You know, I have this strange desire to communicate—commune with you (not like with a spirit but closer than with the word communicate). . . . It is not a strange desire but rather, talking with you in a way that expresses my feelings comes hard to me. At any rate, let me say that I really miss you (YOU) both from a personal point of view (as YOU) and from the point of view of your being the analyst.

Here I go . . .

Let's get this fucking problem out at once . . . I don't want to be the court reporter and will not be. Suffice it to say that the group has its problem with you . . . there is a problem with the way you are viewed, individually and collectively by us. For my part, I seem to be able to handle you as both the analyst, authority, leader . . . and as the member of the group, friend, and man . . . at any time, in any role. I'm not sure that this is not a problem with me. Others in the group are seemingly split. I don't want to define who feels which way, but rather will toss out the points of view as best I can.

Most people in analysis today feel that the analyst will be the one person in whom they can confide, he will hear patiently all of their tzurus (troubles), he will be their confidant, their release, their catalyst . . . he will be FOR THEM!!! If he discusses, reviews, or interprets anything to do with them, he will be a dispassionate, disinterested party. . . . He has no Axe to Grind. This position was the one which you took over the years until recently. You could be relied on to fill this bill.

Now, suddenly, enters the analyst as a person . . . fluctuating in no certain fashion from analyst to member of the group (family) and back again. At first this started slowly on the Tuesday night sessions to which you were invited [alternate sessions usually not attended by group leader]. Then you were yourself more and more on Tuesdays until you pretty much avoided any analytical function on Tuesdays. . . . Then it began to slip over into Thursdays [regular session], little by little, until you were yourself most of the time, and analyst very seldom.

I think that the idea of the Zen Master is a good one. But you do not do this as a technique, but rather for your own purposes. I think that the most clear example, is that of the last session before you left. At the end, you made, as far as I am concerned, a powerful attempt to reach out to Nat and Jill. I think your analysis was brilliant. But I think you failed to reach either of them because your motives were not clean. I feel that you tried to reach them, not for them but for you . . . so that you could keep your family intact waiting for your return. . . . You coldly discarded Martha and tried to salvage Nat and Jill along with the rest of us, excluding Martha. I think I told you that I did not like you for it, and I don't. I do like you for other things, and it is a feeling of friendship which stimulates this letter.

I think the issue is clear. The Zen Master may cause confusion in his adherents while moving from one role to the other, but I feel he cannot possibly succeed if he loses their confidence. His adherence to some higher (disinvolved . . . spiritual?? . . . inwardly peaceful) lights, and his living spirituality seems, in my mind, to keep their confidence. It must be true that some Zen students learn and reach this level and perhaps become Zen Masters themselves sometime.

I feel that if trust and confidence in you is lost by the members of the group that it will disintegrate and die. DOES THE ZEN MASTER SHOW HIS OWN INNER CONFLICTS TO HIS STUDENTS??? DOES HE HAVE INNER CONFLICTS??? IF SO, HOW CAN HE BE THE ZEN MASTER???

I feel like this letter may impose itself upon you while you are on your vacation. . . . That's the good boy in me talking. . . . Fuck it. I'd like to hear from you soon, friend-analyst!!

> Best regards,
> Jack

The only point that needs any explanation is that I had compared the paradoxical communication of the Zen master to his student with my own inconsistent and paradoxical behavior in the group.

This was my answer:

Dear Jack,

I was so happy to receive your letter today. It was a very stimulating one and one that got to the core of the problem in the group and perhaps in man himself. I do not take this problem lightly at all. I am not sure I have the answer or even necessarily that I am on the right track. But what I am doing *feels* right to me. The complete answer to your letter is going to be the book I am writing currently. Incidentally, I would like to include your letter (edited) and my answer to it in my book. However, I will try to give you, as well as I can, my current thinking on some of the issues you raise.

First of all, I think you are right about what you say about my trying to reach Jill and Nat at the last session—at least in part. I think the *motivation* on my part to reach them was stimulated by my wanting very much to keep the family intact. It is unfortunate perhaps that I *needed* this motivation to come up with what I agree was a brilliant analysis of both of them. Perhaps I could have or should have been able to do this scientifically, dispassionately, or lovingly rather than selfishly. But the fact remains that I needed the selfish stimulation to bring the analysis out of me. Also, at that point, I was still quite angry with Martha and either rationally or irrationally (because of my anger) could not make an effort to reach her. I feel somewhat less angry now and perhaps I could reach her. Or perhaps at that point, I could not have reached her anyway, so it would have been a wasted effort.

But let's get back to some of the more crucial points in your letter. You say that, when people go to an analyst, they expect someone who will be for them. My question is this: If the analyst acts in this way, is he not being a partner to their continuing to maintain what is essentially an illusion that our culture perpetuates? There is no one for *you* or for anyone else, ultimately. By not going along with this illusion, the analyst causes the patient to seek his strength inside of himself rather than in perpetuating the search for someone who will really care for him and protect him. Because, even if by some miracle he should find such a person, then he would be insecure and be terribly dependent on that person's survival and in staying in his good graces. It is a false way to try to deal with the problem of aloneness and separateness. My way, though painful, seems to go to the heart of the problem. I am not abdicating my responsibility as your doctor by being "selfish" or self-interested. I am choosing to be this way not because it pleases *me,* but because I feel it is more therapeutic for all of *you* in the long run, even if it may not seem so at any particular moment in time.

The other point you mention seems to be a corollary of this one, though you didn't grasp my explanation of how the Zen master works. The Zen master, in fact, deliberately tries to destroy the confidence of his pupils in him. He does this by presenting them with nonsense, paradoxes, etc. He shows his own helplessness, smallness, and inner conflicts. The fact that he is a master does *not* mean he has risen above having conflicts, but that he can accept them as part of himself without at the same time losing himself. Again, you seem to be seeking someone outside of yourself whom you can *really* trust. There is no such person. And you can only begin to trust *yourself* after you've stopped looking for such a person.

Now let's look at some of the positives. You say you want to commune with me, you do miss me, you do feel like a friend and you also feel free to impose on me even on my vacation. Could all of those things have happened if I had stayed cold, objective, omniscient, "all for you," etc.? It seems to me I would have been a machine and as such been impersonal and a fraud. And could all the other emotional things that have happened in the group have happened if I had stayed in my usual role? Besides, you must remember it was the group that constantly demanded I drop the objective analytic role. Isn't my present role a kind of example to the group of *my* trusting myself and being willing to expose all of my irrationalities with still enough faith not to have to depend on the approval of my patients or their money either? Aren't I taking a bigger risk than anyone else by leaving a safe, secure, rewarding status position for a search for security inside myself?

I don't want your liking me because of my status or skill or education *or* because of any false pictures of my emotional maturity or psychological superiority. This latter would be a fraud and a myth. I also don't want to feel I *have* to have you liking me. I like it very much and I want it, but I cannot attach too much of myself to it, just as you cannot attach too much of yourself to your needing me to be there for you.

Anyway, I'm glad you wrote and I hope you'll feel like writing again to me in Paris. I've felt a great deal closer to you than ever before lately and I value your friendship. What I liked most about your letter was its honesty. If we could only dispense with bullshit! I still can't, but I'm trying.

Give my regards to everyone in the group. You can read this to them if you like, though I didn't write it to them, but to you.

Sincerely,
Dick

All of this leads rather naturally to a discussion about what the goals of psychoanalysis are and how the setting of it—not the theory—either promotes or is counterproductive to these goals. My idea about what distinguishes analytic therapy from supportive therapy is that its focus is self-actualization rather than adaptation or symptom reduction. Abraham Maslow, an American psychoanalyst, wrote a great deal about this concept of self-actualization. Unfortunately, to my mind, he did not present a theory or a process by which this could occur, other than the analyst's focusing on it as a central issue and encouraging the patient's efforts in this direction. While these practices are praiseworthy, I do not think they will have sufficient impact for most patients. A patient has to have his god destroyed before he will stop believing in finding salvation through an idol. The iconoclast can never be the patient—it must be the analyst himself.

People will go to any lengths and suspend all their reality-testing in order to maintain a belief that there is a superior person who can show them the way. Rarely, usually when pushed by a patient or colleague, I have been to astrologers, mystics, and self-appointed gurus myself; I know how strong is the wish to believe them. So many of my patients and so many of my colleagues—bright, educated, scientific people—keep going to card-readers, psychics, self-appointed prophets, and the like. I am sure you would be amazed that I could name easily ten colleagues who have followed these paths rather seriously and continue to do so. So, as I see it, it is my own duty to demystify myself. I cannot expect my patient to do that. It is almost as though the patient wants to become "addicted" to the analyst. With any addiction, the treatment involves some type of forcible disruption of the addictive pattern. The drug-addicted patient needs to be hospitalized because he cannot voluntarily break the pattern. Once the pattern is broken, he may, if he is fortunate, see and experience the advantages of being without his addiction. Then he may be able to continue to relinquish it as an option.

Needing a person to run our lives, help us to cope with reality, take over responsibility for us is the worst and most prevalent kind of human bondage. The classical analytic approach makes a very spurious pretense at avoiding this bond by having the analyst abstinent, anonymous, relatively silent and behind the couch. Freud, however, never saw the analyst's position as a way of preventing this dependent bond. Freud merely happened upon the use of the couch because he started out by doing hypnosis, which required a supine position, and then felt uncomfortable looking at people. He never in any of his theories dealt with this breaking of attachment. But physical separations alone such as the use of the couch do not cure attachments or addictions to *people*. The analyst must help his patients make a connection that is not a dependent one, one in which the patient feels equal and does not look to the analyst for answers and direction or as the possessor of mental health.

Here we must discuss the meaning of the word "dependent." Patients and, sadly, even many therapists fail to distinguish between a need to have another person run one's life and a need for contact, affection, and emotional support. The more we get of the latter, the better off we are. Many people go through their lives with very little of this life-sustaining intimacy. On the other hand, the more we look for and get someone who *takes care* of us, supplies us with goods, makes decisions for us, and who we look up to as our guru or parent, the less capable we feel about ourselves and the lower our self-esteem descends. This distinction between needing intimacy and needing to be taken care of is a crucial one that is largely missing in American psychoanalytic thinking.

I had a bright, attractive patient whom I started seeing in his early twenties and who continued with me intermittently until his middle thirties. His parents, who were very wealthy, supplied him with $50,000 a year for his expenses. He grew fat, indolent, sexually impotent, and was unable to mobilize any kind of effective assertion in any area. He was unable to earn any money—he hardly made a total of $15,000 in the fifteen years I knew him. I and the groups he was in tried hard to help him break the bond with his parents, but he was unable to do so. How can you cure an addict when he lives with a dope pusher? Finally, and luckily for him, in his middle thirties his parents' money ran out. Within two years he was making $200,000 a year in a very competitive business. I use this example because it is a clear and quantitative one of the disadvantages of dependency. Of course, along with his financial success, he became slim, sexually potent, and his self-image rose by light-years.

9

Character Analysis

During the mid-1960s my professional life continued to flourish. I did a great deal of teaching and supervision of other analysts. My practice was excellent. I acquired many bright, interesting, creative patients. A number of them were analysts; some were actors and artists. I enjoy working with people in these fields—they have an access to their unconscious that others sometimes do not. However, I also often treat men or women in other professions, such as law, business, and medicine, who have that same sensitivity. When a patient comes in to see me, I have the privilege of deciding whether to work with this patient myself or refer him or her to a colleague. I can make this decision on the basis of my spontaneous positive reaction or lack of it. Since there are always more people who come to me than I have time to see, I feel extra-ordinarily fortunate. I ask myself during the first session, "Do I wish to spend a part of my life with this person? Is he (or she) interesting enough for me to make an emotional commitment to? Will I consistently look forward to seeing him with anticipation and pleasure? Can I relate easily to the needy child in him, so that I will not be seriously put off by whatever facades he may present? Do I enjoy the facade as well?"

Not every facade is the same. Facades are usually taken over from important figures in our past. Some are interesting; some are not. Some please me; others do not. A facade is as much a part of a person as the needy child is. When I decide quickly—within the first forty-five-minute interview—in the affirmative, I take on the patient. If I do not have this "chemical" response, I reject the patient in a way that does not offend him—by telling him I have no time, or by telling him I think he could do better with a woman analyst, or whatever. This ability to choose, which neither I nor other analysts have at the beginning of their careers, makes my present work a pleasure. I see myself as sitting in a comfortable office and having a group of interesting, bright, talented people come to visit me every day.

I think, whenever possible, it is advisable for an analyst not to treat someone unless he feels a genuine rush of positive feeling toward him or her. It is true that, once we break down defenses and can relate to the vulnerable child in any person—even a murderer—we can feel empathy, compassion, and caring toward that person. Robert Lindner, in his book *Rebel Without a Cause,* did analyze a murderer and was able to experience these positive feelings. However, there are some people we like more than others. This is a function of our particular pasts and of the people who have either been especially good or especially bad to us. I know I am not as likely to be drawn toward men who are like my father and paternal grandfather or to women like my mother and paternal grandmother, as I am toward women like my sister and men who are more like I see myself. No analysts are as "objective" as many people would believe them to be, and a patient's unconscious can always intuit when he as a person is not responded to in an interested, accepting way by the analyst. He can tell if the analyst is delighted to see him. So much of our pain comes from our having been rejected or not responded to positively, that to allow a patient to experience still another situation of this lack of response from his analyst seems cruel and unfortunate. However, at times we analysts do not have such a wide latitude of choice. The situation may be dictated not only by our own financial exigencies but by circumstance. When I was in the Army, I was the only psychiatrist within a fifty-mile radius. A patient on the post had no choice but to see me, nor did I have the option of refusing him. There are many other situations less obvious than this in which the choice is nevertheless limited, such as when one is working in a clinic or organization.

During these years, despite this deep professional satisfaction from my practice, teaching, and supervising, and a reasonable social life and intimate attachment, and even my "enlightenment," I found myself to be despondent much of the time. Instead of being a rebel without a cause, I was a kvetch (complainer) without a cause. So back I went into analysis. This time I was lucky—I really hit the jackpot.

I went to see an English lady in her late forties, whose name I scarcely remember today. She was crisp, cool, and all business; she exhibited very little warmth; but she was exactly what I needed at that stage of my life. She was a follower of the American analyst Edmund Bergler, who wrote a famous book called *The Basic Neurosis* which I had read ten or fifteen years earlier. He also wrote many other books which, in my and many other analysts' opinion, were nothing short of atrocious. Bergler comes across in his books (I have never met him personally) as arrogant, megalomanic, and opinionated. However, he made some points about psychoanalytic theory and practice that helped me considerably both personally and professionally, despite vast disagreements with him in other areas.

Bergler, in a vein that had historical precedent in the work of Wilhelm Reich (before he became a paranoid psychotic), Alfred Adler, and Karen Horney, focused his attention on masochism and the masochistic character. By this he meant psychic suffering as distinguished from the sexual perversion. Unlike myself, he felt that this was not only "the basic neurosis" but almost the sole significant one. I believe that masochism is a very important issue for some patients, but not all. Bergler, like almost every analyst who has made a significant contribution, peremptorily throws out everyone else's work. Bergler described his masochist as a sufferer who always sees the half-empty rather than the half-full glass, who manages to snatch defeat from the jaws of victory, who cannot take "yes" for an answer. So far that fit me perfectly. In addition, he pointed out that the day of every masochist is filled with obsessional worrying about how he made bad decisions in the past which ruined his life and how his future will be beset by untold woes. One of my favorite quotations is: "The greatest tragedies of my life were the ones that never happened." This description also fit me to a tee. In my mind, I had failed every examination I had ever taken and been rejected by every woman I had ever pursued. In fact, I had failed only two examinations in twenty-five years of school. My record of success with women was not quite as sterling, but it was certainly better than my subjective experience of it!

What are the reasons for this "worrying" and suffering? Before even beginning to look at the reasons that are unconscious and complicated, stemming from our early childhood rejections, a superficial reason is that it is a way of trying to elicit sympathetic attention from our environment or from some particular person in it. It is also a way of manipulating people to get them to do our bidding. As long as the suffering is rewarded by the environment, it will persist. The thesis is the same as with my young patient whose indolence was rewarded by his parents' financial support. Freud was very pessimistic about the treatment of psychic masochists. He may well have been! If a masochist is treated in a classical way, he will come in forever to get his analyst's attentive ear to his suffering. Even if the analyst does not gratify him directly by giving him sympathy, at least he lends him what appears to be an attentive ear.

In truth, an analyst who treats a masochistic patient by a classical technique will have a difficult time fighting off boredom and somnolence. Bergler recommended not only a total lack of any sympathy, but a direct attack on the patient's constant attempts to evoke sympathy and to manipulate the therapist through suffering. I had two excellent models of this in my mother and father. My father, who specialized in cardiology, told us that he had a heart block, which threatened his life early. In fact, as I learned in medical school, his block was a congenital anomaly that produced no symptoms or shortening of life; he lived to be eighty-four, always in perfect health until the last year of his life. That was not my father's only manipulation through suffering. He constantly complained of being overworked and not having any leisure time. Of course, that was exactly how he set up his life. And so did I! My mother's and grandmother's sufferings were more quiet, subtle, and passive, but they were very strongly there. My mother always managed to make me feel that I was responsible for her unhappiness and that I could make her happy if I pleased her more. When I was in my late forties, I announced that I was planning to remarry. She did not know or inquire about my intended or the reasons for my decision. She merely said, "You should not do that, Richard." "Why not, Mom?" I said. "Because you have only one mother and it will not make your mother happy," she replied. Now I could see her agenda undisguised. My behavior should be based on only one premise, whether or not it made her happy!

So I had some fine role models for being a sufferer, and certainly as a child I received consistent rewards for my suffering. I could always manipulate my mother, for example—my temper tantrums and my being able to get her to attend the first grade with me attest to that. I also realize that I had a cozy "mutual suffering and sympathy" relationship with her. We both complained about our ill-treatment at the hands of my father and paternal grandfather and gave one another sympathy for it. The women to whom I became attached and even some of the men I befriended were often sympathetic to my woes. I did a great deal of complaining. Sometimes I could make this into a comic routine, which rendered it more bearable, but I am sure that much of the time I must have been a bore.

Well, my new English analyst would not give me a drop. I upped the ante little by little. I even would leave her by saying that this would be my last visit since I was contemplating suicide before my next one. She remained completely unflappable. Finally, when I saw that I could not move her, I began to let go of my suffering. But now comes the saddest tale of all. After about six months in treatment with her in which I had finally found an analyst who understood me well—even too well—she died suddenly. It seemed fate had replayed my childhood experience with my sister. Now I had a real reason to suffer, which I proceeded to do "in spades."

Of course, I sought out another analyst, who was and is an extraordinarily intelligent, warm, sensitive woman. She had had a very difficult life and had a disadvantaged younger brother whom she loved and cared for. When I appeared in her office, she was taken with me, not sexually—she is probably homosexual—but as her unfortunate younger brother. She rewarded my suffering with sympathy and kindness. I have never suffered so much as I did in the year I was in treatment with her. At the end of that year, I was in an extended group called a marathon with her as the leader and several of my colleagues as participants. During the marathon, my colleagues pointed out to her that her treatment of me was as if she were responding to a disadvantaged younger brother. "But," she said "Richard *is* my brother." This was an involuntary slip that shocked all of us, including her and myself. She had been involved in such a strong countertransference to me that she could hardly distinguish me from her brother.

I still have the greatest respect for her dedication and her integrity, as I do for Dr. Silverberg's. I do not mention her name because, despite being a victim of her countertransference—and almost a suicide—I bear her no illwill. She felt truly guilty and repentant and admitted her error. The finest of us can become involved in these situations. I remain friendly with her and have even referred patients to her. My experience with her plus my previous good work with my English analyst finally gave me the strength to leave her and with that to abandon a good deal of my masochism. I realized that the suffering I went through was not worth the reward of sympathy I received.

The two analytic experiences with these women were also extremely important for my growth as a therapist. Many patients present serious masochistic problems. I learned "the hard way" never to indulge them or to allow myself to be manipulated. Of course, manipulation by suicidal threat is a very difficult issue for an analyst to handle. Early in my career, I found it hard to distinguish between the possibility of a genuine attempt and a manipulation. My rule of thumb is that if there is the remotest chance of a real attempt, it is better to be safe than sorry. Analysts are not effective at treating dead patients. When I have an established relationship with a patient and he or she is talking about contemplating suicide, I make the patient give me a solemn promise that he will call me before taking any irreversible step. With such a patient I can trust him to keep his word. When I feel sure the patient is using a suicidal threat as a way of manipulating me, then I lend the same deaf ear to him that my English analyst did to me.

This whole area is obviously very tricky because we are dealing with life and death. We must not rule out the possibility of personal error. This is one area in which I strongly advise consultation with an experienced colleague if there is any question in the analyst's mind. During this period of my life—in the late sixties—I had my only experience of a patient in treatment committing suicide. She was a new patient whom I had seen only a few times and she had never mentioned the possibility of suicide. Still, the experience for me was devastating and shattering. Perhaps with greater wisdom or experience, it could have been avoided. I certainly do not envy neurosurgeons, who lose a relatively high percentage of their patients.

One aspect of masochism in which I have been especially interested is what lay people call "worrying." This is so ubiquitous that most people regard it as part of their personality and everyone else's. Going over past mistakes or failures, being down on oneself for real or imagined lacks, and predicting grave events in the future seems "normal." In fact, this is a symptom we analysts call "masochistic obsessions." If one thinks clearly about the issue, the only time frame the mind should be in is the present. The past is gone and the future does not need to be dealt with until it arrives. Existentialists make the point that the only time is now. But a worrier's obsessions keep him from ever being totally in the present. I used to be plagued by these obsessions. I would be sitting treating a patient, but simultaneously I would have a tape playing in my head: "When you leave this office, you may have a flat tire. You will call the Auto Club and they won't appear for hours. Your wife will never believe your story, but will accuse you of infidelity," and so on. After a day filled with this kind of assault, the person has no choice but to be depressed.

Helping patients to identify these obsessions and attempt to suppress them is part of an overall treatment of psychic masochism. The early roots do have to do with rage against depriving or restricting parents, that is turned against the self. But the characterological issues of seeking sympathy and attention and being able to manipulate through suffering must be addressed first. Many analysts, in my opinion, do not put enough stress on the necessity of attacking the secondary gains (rewards) through manipulation that the psychic masochists enjoy. A very classical free association technique might well arrive at the deepest roots of masochism as primitive rage against mother that is turned against the self. Wilhelm Reich, in his book *Character Analysis*, in fact describes such a patient, who understood all of the deepest roots of his masochism but remained exactly the same. Reich stressed the need to attack the character defenses before uncovering the unconscious roots.

Since my mother, my father, and I were all immersed in

psychic masochism, I have been especially sensitive—not altogether in a positive way—to patients who have this problem. Also, my own two opposite experiences as a patient, one very helpful and the other very destructive, enlightened me about the value of not rewarding the psychic masochist's suffering with sympathy.

10

The English Psychoanalysts

In the late sixties a patient of mine, also an analyst, recommended a book by an English analyst I had never heard of, Harry Guntrip. The rather cumbersome title was *Schizoid Phenomena, Object Relations and the Self*—enough to frighten even a hardened psychoanalyst. But the ideas in it were so compelling that I felt Dr. Guntrip had written about me. On finishing the book, I sat down and wrote him a letter saying that I wanted to come over to England and have him analyze me. He answered that he had been sickly and was really not prepared to take on any new patients. He died a few years later. So I had to try to digest and utilize the material in the book without the benefit of his personal presence.

First of all, some translations from "analese." The English use of the word "schizoid" differs from the American usage. The Americans use it to signify a loner, a person who is very cut off, an isolate. The English use it to mean someone who is cut off, but only from intimacy. Such a person may be very affable, have many acquaintances, be married and have children, and be very good at social intercourse; but he is unable to involve himself or sustain a really deep intimate attachment. I think it is no accident that attention to these phenomena arose in England. Many English people as well as their WASP American descendants suffer from this problem. "Object relations" is another term that requires translation, this time from "analese" via "English English" and also German. Freud, after he rejected his seduction theory, constantly used the words "investing an object with libido." This is the kind of phrase that personally repels me. All it

110

really means is putting your love into another person. "Object" here simply means person, although it is the antithesis of the way the word "object" is used by us in common parlance. When we make a person into a sex object, for instance, we mean that we dehumanize them. "Object" as used here means the opposite—a human person. So the phrase "object relations" merely means interpersonal relations.

Now that I have hopefully gotten past some of the semantics, let me get into what it was in Guntrip's book that "knocked my socks off." Freud and his followers stuck to and still stick to an instinct theory. Freud started out his thinking very much along interpersonal lines. His early cases are explained by the neurosis coming from some childhood trauma—not infrequently a sexual seduction. Freud checked over his data and either could not or would not believe these seductions could have taken place by fathers or other male relatives in these upstanding families. In fact, historically such seductions were not so uncommon then, nor are they in America today. But also many of them were in truth the patients' fantasies rather than fact. This proved a tremendous blow to Freud's belief system. So he dropped the theories of "childhood experience and personal destiny" (the title of Silverberg's book, incidentally) and moved to the libido theory. In my opinion, this move, which occurred around the turn of the century, dealt a major blow to psychoanalysis from which it has just begun to recover.

Much has been written recently about the controversy over Freud's giving up his seduction theory. Included in this controversy have been many personal attacks on Freud for allegedly falsifying reports on his patients in order to prove his theories. Aside from these rather foolish ad hominem attacks, the theoretical and historical points about Freud giving up his seduction theories are extremely important. When Freud first started seeing patients around the turn of the century, he felt that the basis of their neurotic problems had to do with unfortunate experiences they had had in childhood, especially sexual seductions. He subsequently found that many if not all of those seductions had not occurred in fact but were usually fantasies of the patient. He was so disillusioned by his discoveries that he gave up the idea that neurosis was caused by traumatic childhood experiences and placed the causality on the patient's fantasies. In the process his focus became intrapsychic rather than interpersonal. From this he developed the libido theory, which put emphasis of the cause of neurosis on the way the patient handled his instinctual energy rather than on difficulties arising from the patient's life experience.

Following this lead, classical analysts in their treatment have sought to uncover the patient's fantasy and have placed little emphasis on the real relationship between the patient and his family members or between the patient and his analyst. The classical analyst's role has appropriately been to stay in the background. If, however, the patient's problems have, in fact, been caused by traumatic childhood experiences with significant figures, then the role of the analyst would be perceived in a quite different way. Then his role would be to provide the patient with a "corrective emotional experience" that might make up for lacks in his development and decondition him to traumatic events of his childhood.

After Freud left his interpersonal views, he began to think of people's problems as stemming from instinctual energies (libido) that sought gratification and were thwarted in the process. He was attracted to the work that was being done at that time in the physical sciences—especially the work in physics involving the distribution of energy. Freudians think of people's troubles as being based on instincts seeking gratification, and the vicissitudes of this process. The English Object Relations analysts think of people needing people rather than instincts needing gratification. This is obviously oversimplified, but it does contain the essence of the difference. The English analysts—the most important of whom are Melanie Klein, John Bowlby, W. R. D. Fairbairn, Donald Winnicott, Wilfred Bion, Harry Guntrip, and Hanna Segal—focused their attention on the need an infant has for attachment to his mother and the difficulties that can arise in the process of attachment.

This focus, first of all, gets rid in one fell swoop of all the semantic gobbledegook that was transferred from physics into psychology, such as libidinization of the anus, counter-cathexis, and the like. Secondly, it deals with issues that are part of our daily experiences. We do have a need for an intimate attachment. We *are* afraid we will be rejected because of our real or imagined deficiencies. We are also afraid to make an emotionally intimate attachment for fear of the pain we may suffer if we should ever lose it. And we are afraid to make such an attachment because it might be so compelling that we would turn ourselves over to the person we connect to and thus lose our autonomy and our Selves. Now these are real feelings we can all identify. This is psychology, not physics.

Many of us are so frightened of any or all of these eventualities that we lock the little needy baby in us up in a vault, to use one of Guntrip's metaphors. We are so frightened to risk some of the consequences of seeking the intimacy we need that we spend much or, for some people, all of our lives in a cold isolation. But this isolation is not a totally numb one. People always have some idea of what they need and sense that they are not getting their needs met—"All men lead lives of quiet desperation." But their fear prevents them from seeking out the very thing that could relieve their pain and loneliness. Practically none of us as infants got the amount of intimacy that our psycho-biological needs require. This may be a fact of life, that the attachment period human infants require is just not possible in our modern world, which tends to shorten the period during which mothers can be totally devoted to their infants. So we all go through our lives with a terrible hunger for this attachment and a terrible despair about ever getting it.

But, of course, there are vast quantitative differences in the amount of intimacy individuals receive. It is understood that when I speak of intimacy, I am not talking about sex. I am talking about allowing oneself to be a vulnerable baby and to be held, stroked, and comforted by another person. Freud and his followers put the emphasis on sexual needs. Nowadays I do not often run into a patient who is sexually deprived; however, I rarely run into one who feels emotionally cherished. I remember when I finished Guntrip's book, I said to myself that finally I understood what I had been missing in my life. The ten analysts I had had up to that point did not have the slightest clue as to what it was. This man three thousand miles away in the unlikely town of Leeds, England, understood more about me than my ten analysts combined. I turned to my lover, explained my discovery, and asked her to give me the kind of succor I needed. She was very intelligent and comprehended completely what I needed; she also was a person of great integrity. She responded by saying that she wished she could fulfill my needs, but—knowing herself—there was no way she ever could. We decided to part that day without acrimony. Now that I finally knew what I wanted, I was certainly not going to stay with someone who, despite her many assets, could not properly provide it for me. She was just not the kind of person who felt comfortable holding me, comforting me, or being affectionate in that way.

A theme I developed later in a book I co-authored, *Big You—Little You,* is that we all have a needy baby in us that coexists with the functioning adult. These two parts of us are by no means mutually exclusive. I can see patients all day long, run a large clinic, handle my finances, and yet at night can choose to suspend my effective adult and become a vulnerable baby who needs to be held, stroked, and comforted. Luckily I have found a person who can provide this; but obviously I spent the major portion of my life not ever knowing what I needed. So I was hardly able to allow my-self to ask for it and clearly was not seeking the sort of person who could provide it. In my opinion, this is what we all need, but how many people do we know who can begin to acknowledge it? Does this not sound like a better idea about what makes people angry, frustrated, and de-spairing than the frustration of their sexual needs? Who in today's society after the sexual revolution and the women's liberation movement and sex therapy is *that* frustrated sex-ually?

The main focus of this kind of analysis, then, is off the sexual competition with father for mother, or vice versa (which certainly exists), and on to the mother–child dyad, especially in the first year of life. Certainly the Industrial Revolution and the need for women to be wage earners (along with many other cultural factors) cut into the amount of mothering a child could get. But what about the specific deficits in the mothering response? Bowlby, another En-glish analyst, who lately has been well received in the United States, has written extensively on the process of at-tachment and the reaction to separations. There are many different circumstances that can interfere with the process of attachment. The child can be premature and require an in-cubator; the child can be sick; the child can have a genetic defect that interferes or a constitution that does not accept mothering easily. He may have colic.

Then, too, the mother may be physically ill. My mother, for example, developed a lung disease when I was four months old; this abrupt weaning undoubtedly contributed to my fear of abandonment. A mother like mine may be very insecure and unable to give mothering in a relaxed manner. She may be preoccupied with internal issues—such as postpartum depression. She may have difficulties with her husband or have another child that is sick or disadvan-taged. There are many, many kinds of problems in child or mother or family or in the specific subculture that prevent adequate mothering. It seems as if there may be more people in our society who do not get these early needs met than those who do.

Finally, even if these needs are met fairly adequately (Winnicott's phrase is "good enough mothering"), circumstances—fire, flood, war, death, illness—can come along to cause a disruption, as occurred for me at four months. René Spitz, the American psychoanalyst, studied the effect of infants who had "good enough mothering" for the first six months but who were then put in foundling homes in which only their physical nurturing needs and medical needs were taken care of adequately; emotional nurturing was not provided. The infants went through phases of rage, depression, and then apathy. Their total beings were so traumatized that many became subject to infections and as many as a quarter of them were dead by the end of the first year. This is a quite remarkable statistic. One can imagine the effects of traumata not quite so dramatic. In fact, I know too well the effects, since I was the victim of a combination of inadequate mothering plus a sudden disruption of all mothering in the first year. In addition, the intimate loving connection I did have with my sister was very abruptly terminated at age seven by her death. No wonder I thought Guntrip was writing about me! And even though I had a very difficult Oedipal situation, it did not have half the impact of the early traumata. "As the twig is bent, so grows the tree." The earlier the trauma, the greater the impact. In fact, I have treated a patient who had the most obvious Oedipal situation: her father had overt sexual contact with her from ages nine to eighteen. Yet her inadequate mothering had caused her a great deal more grief than her incestuous relationship with her father. She feels insecure and unlovable, and spends most of her life compulsively trying to please the people around her, searching for good mothering. I have also seen patients who had many years of incestuous experiences with their older brothers, who were not tremendously disturbed because they had had "good enough mothering."

But not enough mothering or abruptly terminated mothering are not the only possible dangers in the process of attachment. The quality and quantity of the mothering are also crucial. There are some mothers who make a child into a narcissistic extension of themselves. They do not react to him as if he were a separate person. My grandfather—my substitute mother—did this with me. I did not exist for him except to relive his life. One of my patients said her mother used to say of her, "You are my right arm." The classical stage mother in *Gypsy* wanted her daughter to achieve the fame that she herself had not attained. Some mothers of this ilk cannot distinguish realistic differences in constitution and personality or even gender between themselves and their child. They may treat a boy as if he were a girl. When the mother is hungry, she may feel the child is hungry and feed him. This lack of ability to differentiate can cause the child's Self—the part that is unique to him—to be obliterated.

Freudians believe there is no self at birth and that the ego (the executive part of the mind) develops out of an undifferentiated mass of instincts (id). They do not use the concept of Self—the totality of an individual—but divide him into id (instincts), ego (executive part), and superego (conscience). Object Relations analysts believe a child is born with a Self, a whole idiosyncratic personality. Observation of infants as well as many psychological research studies have tended to confirm the latter view. Infants are very different from one another from birth onward. They can tell the difference between their mother and another person even at two weeks of age. A mother who does not recognize her child as different from herself will not be able to respond empathically to him, since there will be a blurring of boundaries between herself and the child as separate entities.

Another kind of mother is the possessive mother who holds onto the child for dear life to satisfy her own needs rather than being empathic to what the child really needs. For these mothers, the children are not narcissistic extensions but need-fulfilling objects—suppliers. Then there are mothers who are overtly hostile and rejecting to their infants for a variety of reasons. One mother I treated said she hated her daughter from the word "go" because she resembled her hated mother-in-law.

To make it simple—perhaps simplistic—some of us have not enough mothering, others of us have too much of the wrong kind. Some of us who are really unfortunate have not had enough when we needed it and too much when we did not. These poor people are the classical schizoids (in the English sense). They are involved in what is known as a double approach–avoidance reaction. This is not as complicated as it sounds. When they do not have a secure attachment, they suffer terribly from the lack of it. When on the other hand they do have one, they suffer from a fear of losing themselves, their identity and autonomy, in the other person, or of being taken over by the other person. They bounce back and forth between Scylla and Caribdis; they "can't live with them and they can't live without them." To my mind, trying to treat such a person without having a knowledge of Object Relations theory is impossible. Yet Freudian analysts attempt to treat these people in the usual classical manner, using free association while totally rejecting Object Relations theory. But even if they accepted the theory, how could you treat a person's fear of intimacy while sitting behind him while he is lying on the couch? The very nature of classical technique precludes the possibility of intimacy. It is not just the physical position of the analyst; it is his silence, his anonymity and overall stance. And, all too often, it is his *own* fear of or choice against intimacy with a patient. Let me give an example.

Alice, aged thirty-nine, came to see me on a consultation. I supervised the work of the therapist she was seeing. Her therapist, a bright, well-trained, competent analyst, had not been able to move her from a routine of talking about her problems with her husband and children. The husband was a remote, obsessional man, who was extremely male-chauvinistic in his orientation to his, and her, role in the marriage. She got very little of anything from him, and reasonably good sex but little else from a lover she had. Her children had a variety of problems that obsessed the patient.

When I saw her, she reached me tremendously with what seemed to be an extraordinarily strong sense of desperation and an almost palpable need to be held like a baby. I told her of my impression of her and my emotional reponse of wanting to hold her in the first consultation. She was the kind of person who was very defensive about acknowledging or showing her need, but it was clear that I had reached her. I knew that her therapist did not, and could not, have the same deep communication with her, and I regretted not being able to treat her; but I told her that perhaps she might enter one of my groups and that I would discuss her problems with her therapist. In my discussions with the therapist, and in the patient's discussions with her, it became clear to all three of us that I should be seeing her in individual therapy. I arranged to see her once a week and shortly thereafter twice a week.

The focus of our discussions was always on the relationship between us. I would handle her discussion about anything else as a resistance against involvement with me, and ask her to concentrate on her feelings at the moment and especially on any feelings she might have about me. Her relationship to me was characterized by the movement in and out that is so typical of "schizoid" people. She would allow herself a brief awareness of a need to be closer to me—either to touch me or to move physically close to me or a wish to be held by me—and then she would become frightened and look around the room at the paintings, or talk about her husband and children, or anything other than the "I and thou." I would consistently analyze this as a defense against some fear of closeness. Very, very gradually she allowed herself to acknowledge a wish to sit closer to me, or wish to touch me. My position was that it was very realistic and very appropriate for her to have these wishes and to want to gratify them. I also had to convey strongly to her that I was very amenable to gratifying all of these wishes and it was her own blocks and fears that prevented her gratification. Gradually and tentatively she allowed herself to touch my hand—she still in her armchair and I in mine. (As I have said, I no longer use the couch except in rare circumstances. If we conceptualize a particular patient's psychological problems in terms of fears of intimacy that arise in the first year of life, then the use of the couch is more of a continuation of a schizoid defense on the part of the analyst and/or the patient than it is a procedure that aids resolution of problems.)

After a while, the issue of sitting next to me on the couch arose in Alice's fantasies. One must understand that Alice was a very shy, inhibited person, who had tremendous problems asking anyone for anything. The same request by a devouring hysterical patient who was manipulating the analyst might very correctly be refused. But every move toward me, or request of me, by Alice was fraught with great anxiety. Finally we decided we would sit next to one another on the couch. Again my role was that of a "good first-year-of-life mother," who was delighted to gratify as many infantile needs as she could ask for, but would not "read her mind" about what her needs were, and would try to keep any needs of my own out of the treatment unless they were so overpowering that they would interfere. In such cases I told Alice that I would verbalize what was going on inside myself. I also told her that I did not in any way pretend I did not have the same kind of needs that she did. I was "ahead" of her only in being able to acknowledge them without shame and in being very clear on the importance of gratifying them to my general sense of wellbeing.

Alice gradually began to get more in touch with a need to be held, and she allowed herself to be held by me. With this came the feeling that she would be considered to be physically loathsome by me; this especially focused on the feeling that her breath would be offensive. Incidentally, I have found in almost all instances in which I have used this approach to therapy that the idea of smelling bad has been a central issue at this point to the fears of closeness. There is a basic, almost paranoid belief in very many of us that we smell badly and that this means that attempts on our own part to get close to another person will inevitably be rejected. It is one of the first issues that appears in this technique of treatment. How could this extremely important issue appear with its full force if the patient is on the couch and the analyst is behind him/her? It may appear, but not with anything like its full force.

Alice tried to handle her fear by chewing gum and mints before and during our sessions; eventually she understood the meaning of this and was able to stop it. Alice was not in any way loathsome. Neither is any baby, or any adult who is presenting his or her baby Self to us for our maternal response. Gradually she began to feel less loathsome, and as if she could be acceptable to me (or to someone else). She allowed herself the feeling of being able to be physically close to another person.

At this point, she very hesitatingly and in a most embarrassed way said that her closeness to me brought up sexual feelings in her. The handling of this situation is extremely important when using this form of treatment. I had to acknowledge that there were sexual feelings in her that this closeness brought out and that there was nothing wrong with these feelings. However, I told her that these feelings were essentially a defense against more infantile feelings of need. As uncomfortable as her sexual feelings toward me may have made her, her infantile feelings of need were much more threatening and made her feel much more vulnerable. I told her to be sure to report the appearance of any sexual feelings, but that they were essentially a defense against earlier, much more frightening, kinds of anxiety. This worked very well at that point and at the two or three other times when these feelings appeared. In fact, after this the sexual feelings hardly ever appeared.

One might imagine that sexual feelings on the part of either the patient or the analyst could constitute a major stumbling block in the use of this kind of treatment, and in truth it might for some analysts. From the point of view of the patient, he or she will understand the nature of the relationship as a reliving of the mother–child dyad during the first year of life. If the analyst is not involved in a countertransference, the patient will respond very well to the interpretation of the sexual feelings as a defense against greater fears and vulnerability. In my experience with using this technique, this has never constituted a major problem.

If there is a problem, its roots will probably rest in the therapist. Here, too, there are many factors that militate in favor of reducing, if not totally extinguishing, any sexual feelings the therapist might have toward the patient. The nature of the whole transaction before them is so clearly in an infant–mother modality that there is a mind-set in the therapist against anything sexual. Then hopefully the therapist will be mature enough to have his sexual needs gratified elsewhere and to have the welfare of his patient so clearly and prominently in mind that the possibility of using or exploiting the patient sexually, or even consciously desiring to do so, will be very remote. However, there could very well be therapists who, on the basis of their knowledge of themselves or their external situation, may not trust themselves to avoid sexual behavior or even very strong sexual desires. This would certainly be extremely destructive to a patient. Anyone who is not totally sure that he can trust himself in this way should not engage in this kind of therapy.

Now let us get back to Alice. She has gotten past her feeling of being physically loathsome; she has gotten past her tendency to sexualize the relationship; she has begun to allow herself to ask for something from a person and even to take in the pleasure from it. But all of a sudden she "turns off"—going once again into a schizoid position. What is it now? Gradually it emerges that she is afraid of allowing herself these pleasures because if she ever lost me, she would be devastated by the loss. What can be done about this? Slowly she realized that her ability to "get" was not determined by my presence, but by her own awareness of her needs and the priority she gave to their satisfaction. There will always be someone around to respond to her if she is free to recognize her need, acknowledge it, and ask another human being to gratify it. Most people enjoy responding to being asked to gratify these kinds of needs. True, there are people who do not, but they hardly constitute a majority.

So another hurdle is bridged. The patient's distancing maneuvers are diminished and she starts to feel close again. But now once again her schizoid defenses reappear. She begins to talk about "outside problems." She looks out of the window; she feels uncomfortable about coming and begins to think of leaving treatment. At this point we are beginning to come into contact with what is the greatest fear of all: the fear that if she allows herself to get close to me, she will merge with me and lose her identity and her autonomy.

Sometimes these fears are first projected in a paranoid way. The patient believes that what I really want is to render her totally helpless and then take her over and impose my will on her. We examine this possibility seriously. What is there in it for me? I might be able to enslave her, but this is not something that would please or gratify me. And even if I wanted to do this, she could resist it. Then what is the real problem? It emerges that it is her *wish* to be merged with me. She tells me a dream: She is in a country that is being invaded. The troops are marching through the streets. There is a stairway leading up to her house. She puts a few knives on the first landing and some cameras on the second landing as if magically they will halt the invaders, but these measures do not work. The invaders keep coming. She runs up to the attic and hides in a closet.

We talk about this dream as we have about many of Alice's dreams. This is a typical one. She has a wish to be invaded by another person and is unsure of her boundaries.

She tries to use her hostility to ward off the invader (the knives), but it does not work. What do the cameras mean? She says they represent her being an observer and recorder in a scene rather than a participant. So the cameras represent her being with another person but remaining detached. This does not work either. Her wish to be invaded destroys her own sense of her own boundaries. Any contact with a person becomes fraught with danger. Finally, she retreats into a closet—a totally cut-off position where real outside boundaries relieve her of her anxiety about the stability of her ego boundaries. She is also in the attic. This might be part of the secondary elaboration of the dream (perhaps borrowed from Anne Frank), or might be a reference to another defense of hers, intellectualization—using the top part of her body, her head.

In the same session in which she describes her dream, Alice tells me of feeling very badly when a man called her up and asked her to go out to dinner and she accepted. She did not really like this man and was not attracted to him, but she found herself doing what he wanted and going against her own wishes. After she accepted, she felt a deadness and a confusion. When she went out with him, she felt as if she was not really there, but was just going through the motions of being there.

Alice worked through all these problems, and their ramifications, over and over in treatment. She got in touch with all of her fears about closeness in the therapeutic but real situation with me. The fears diminished and she managed to get closer to the people she encountered. Gradually she was able to ask her husband for the things she really needed from him; unfortunately, he was unable to give them to her. In time she left her marriage, met a very warm, affectionate man, married him and, as far as I can determine, is getting along very well with him and feeling quite happy most of the time.

Not every patient with this problem has the same response as Alice. Some require a much longer analysis of their defenses before this kind of treatment can be considered. I would say, however, that almost all of the patients I have treated in this way have had a marked diminution of their anxiety about closeness and, along with this, an improvement in the quality of their relatedness to other people, including their most intimate relationships.

My treatment of such a patient is my own. It derives from theory, but it has not been described by any of the well-known theorists. When I decide to treat such a patient, I first of all never accept him or her unless I know I have a desire for intimacy with that particular person. I also have to be certain that I have no emotional bars in myself against that intimacy, even though I may have the conscious desire for it. Then I can genuinely present myself as someone with whom he or she has the *possibility* of intimacy. Of course, he may not choose to be intimate with me as a matter of personal taste. If that is so and he has a schizoid problem, he will very likely seek another analyst. If *he* is available for intimacy by his choice and he can see that I put no bars in the way of it, then he can get to understand what he does to avoid it. Our focus of attention is totally on the dyad between us. The introduction of other material, except to substantiate insights derived from our relationship, is dealt with as a resistance.

Resistance is not just the avoidance of the material, but avoidance of the closeness he could have and desires to have with me. So if he looks away or moves away or starts off a session in an aloof position, this must be analyzed by me as a defense against a fear of closeness. When this defense is attacked persistently and consistently enough, the patient will begin to reveal his expectation of rejection if he comes close. Many of these fears focus on general unattractiveness and a poor body image. But as with Alice, most frequently they become fixed on being bad-smelling. Now, of course, these patients do not smell badly. I think one of the first feelings of rejection an infant must experience is from his mother's attitude toward changing his diapers. When these fears are conceptualized and tied in by dreams, associations, or memories with his infancy and childhood, the patient is relieved and moves closer. Incidentally, "closer" can and often does mean physically closer. It may at that point mean moving his chair nearer, or it may mean sitting next to me on the couch.

After resting on his laurels for having overcome his fears of rejection, the patient again stays away or moves away. Again, his defenses are attacked. After a while, he says he would like to get close to me but fears that if he does, I might die or leave him or the treatment might end and he might lose me. In turns, this may evoke dreams and lifting of repression. He may recall having been left by his mother and the subsequent despair and pain he suffered. He does not want to risk that again. Next, he comes to see that he is in a different position now than he was in his childhood, when he was totally dependent on his mother. If he lost me, he would suffer but he would have the wherewithal to replace me after a mourning period. Once more having conquered this fear, he begins to feel more comfortable and to allow himself to feel closer to me. But soon another dread arises. What if I want to possess him, take him over, control him? Will he lose his autonomy and Self and become a mere extension of me? He recalls instances of his mother's possessiveness toward him and her control of him. Am I like his mother?

We must examine this issue seriously. I might be. Certainly, some analysts are possessive of their patients. Even Mr. Integrity, Dr. Silverberg, apparently was possessive of Montgomery Clift. I am not automatically exempt from that possibility in general or in particular toward this patient. We examine my relationship toward him and we conclude that I have not been like his mother. We have climbed up onto a new plateau of comfort and ability to be close. Is this the end of the trail? Is he now home free—free to be close to me and then subsequently to be able to be so with someone else of his choice? Alas, this is not the case. Once more he withdraws. I attack his defense. What can it be now? He comes to realize that even if *I* am not possessive, *he* has a wish to be possessed, bound, enmeshed. Even without my attempting to ensnare him, even with my complete refusal to participate in this kind of relationship, so strong is *his* need for a merged connection that he feels he will surrender himself to me and then be lost as an autonomous person.

This problem is a bit more difficult. I must help him to go through a process in which he does merge with me, but then gradually separates and develops boundaries. How can I do it? What is the theory to help me? Luckily—just in the nick of time—a theory arrives upon the analytic scene in America to rescue both the patient and myself from this dilemma.

11

Ego Psychology:
Separation-Individuation

During the late 1960s and early 1970s the work of Margaret
Mahler, a foreign-born psychoanalyst who did most of her
work in America, began to influence the analytic scene in
America. She was a member of the classical analytic school,
but much of her work was based on observation of infants
and children. In that sense she bridged a gap between
Oedipal classicism and the child-developmental perspective
of the Object Relations school. However, true to the analytic tradition of knowing all the answers and not sharing
credit with anyone, neither of these schools—Mahler and
Object Relations—recognizes one another. As a matter of
fact, there are still many members of the classical analytic
school who do not recognize Mahler's work and who think
of it as a deviation (this sounds like Communist doctrine,
does it not?).

I have met Dr. Mahler, who is now in her seventies. She
is a rather crusty, imperious woman. I remember her sitting
in a central chair at a party and—like a queen—expecting
her subjects to come over to her and pay obeisance. Despite
my dislike of her pose, I will gladly be one of those to kneel
and kiss her ring. She has made an enormous contribution
to the field in describing *The Psychological Birth of the Human
Infant,* which is the title of one of her books. Lately there
has been considerable dispute about the validity of her ob-
servations, especially for the first months of life; nevertheless, her conclusions are so useful clinically that one can
forgive a great deal. What Mahler has done is to describe the

developmental process of a newborn infant from isolation to a merged kind of attachment to the mother, and then through the subsequent stages that lead—or unfortunately often do not lead—to a free, independent person.

According to Mahler, when the infant is first born and throughout the early weeks of his life, he experiences himself and his surrounding world as one. He does not differentiate himself from the outside world, "inner" from "outer." Mahler calls this the "autistic" phase. Of course, Object Relations theory contradicts this, saying that even from the beginning an infant experiences a separate Self that seeks contact with the mother. But this is too much quibbling about theory for our purposes. In any case, Mahler sees children with Infantile Autism as fixated at this stage, which means that these rare unfortunate children can never progress beyond this stage—not even to form an attachment to their mother. The next phase she describes is called the stage of "symbiosis" between mother and child. The concept of symbiosis is one of the most useful in modern psychoanalytic theory. Mahler took the word from botany, where it describes the interdependent relationship between two organisms, in which neither can survive without the other. In Mahler's scheme, the symbiotic phase is the closest kind of bonding or merging between mother and child. Here the child *and the mother* experience themselves as one. And here we see a connection between Mahler's theory and the need for attachment as described by the English psychoanalysts.

According to Mahler, too, it is essential for an infant to have the kind of mother who will allow and even welcome and delight in this bonding with her. Perhaps I may have been fortunate enough to get this very early connection with my mother. If a person does not have this, it will be very difficult for him to move easily through the rest of the cycle and toward becoming a relatively independent person. People who did not have enough of this bonding or merging in their infancy tend to look for it in an anachronistic way the rest of their lives. Often when they do attach, they become merged with the other person and lose their autonomy. Or they may be so afraid of this tendency in themselves—like our English schizoid—that they avoid intimacy for the rest of their lives.

Some people who remain permanently fixated at this level are psychotic, especially schizophrenic. The important clinical issue here is for the therapist to recognize a person who is permanently fixated at this level and not to push him into a phase of independence he is not able to achieve. He may be able to move laterally into a better symbiotic connection, but not vertically toward independence. I have in the past made the mistake of encouraging people at this level to leave the person with whom they had a symbiotic bond without having another such possible connection at hand. It proved a serious mistake. The patient failed in his attempt and his self-esteem was lowered.

The next phase is that of separation-individuation. Mahler breaks this down into three stages: differentiation, practicing, and rapprochement. The differentiation is divided into physical and psychological categories. By "physical differentiation" is meant the infant's ability to distinguish between parts of his own body and those of his mother (and later on, his partner). This seems relatively elementary, but sometimes in a warm embrace with an intimate, we can even momentarily lose this power—we do not know whether the hand we are holding is our own or our partner's. "Psychological differentiation" is the infant's ability to distinguish his own ideas and feelings from those of his mother. Psychological differentiation is something all of us tend to lose at times in close relationships. We are fuzzy about whether we are doing something because we wish to or because we think our mate wishes us to. Even my well-functioning patients, and certainly I myself, get stuck in this phase at times. "You want an ice-cream cone, don't you, honey?" I say. "No," my wife replies, "It is *you* who wants an ice-cream cone." People who are relatively well functioning neurotics often fall back into this way of relating.

The next stage is "practicing." The infant crawls and later walks away from his mother. He is excited by his freedom and the discoveries he makes during his explorations. But every once in a while, he needs to return to mother, touch base, and "refuel." When a patient is in the process of breaking away from a relationship or a job, he does not need a silent, anonymous analyst. He needs—as a toddler does—a figure who encourages his ventures into new territory. He needs an analyst who understands what gap in his childhood he is currently filling. He also needs one who, especially at this point when his ventures are quite tentative, is constantly available for "refueling," touching base for support before venturing out again.

I encourage the patients' adventures. I also encourage them to call me at any time, day or night, if they need to touch base with me. This brings up one of the continuing controversies I have had with analysts of a more classical persuasion. One of Dr. Mahler's devoted followers is Dr. Gertrude Blanck. She and her husband, Reuben, have written two of the finest books on the theories of ego psychology and the application of Dr. Mahler's principles. Gertude, I think by any standards, is a pretty reserved woman. She and I have had some interesting debates on the issue of abstinence versus gratifying the patient. I remember once we debated publicly on the advisability of offering a cup of coffee to a patient who had come in from the cold, had not had a chance to have breakfast, and requested some coffee. Our debate over the cup of coffee is still talked about at the Long Island Consultation Center, where it occurred in the early seventies. It is a very important issue in the theory of technique in psychoanalysis and one in which I must admit that there is something to be said on both sides.

Gertude Blanck and other classically oriented analysts argue that giving this patient a cup of coffee impedes the separation from the analyst, the figure the patient has chosen for his or her bonding. Along similar lines, they say that giving the patient the coffee fosters the illusion that the patient can find his sustenance in the analyst and does not need to seek it for himself or from some other figure. Also, the refusal of coffee—if it is requested by the patient—can be useful in therapy, as it can evoke some primitive rage from his childhood at being denied or deprived, which can then be explored in the therapeutic setting. Further, offering the coffee could be part of a tacit agreement between patient and therapist to avoid such feelings and to continue a dependent bond. The therapist could then become what I like to call "a chicken soup therapist" rather than an analyst, and the therapy a supportive Band-Aid rather than a deeply creative analytic process. The giving of the coffee might also tend to avoid exploration of the deeper meaning of the patient's request. For example, this patient may really be saying, "I feel deprived by you. Your interpretations are worthless. I need you to give me something. At least I can get a cup of coffee from you." Another issue is whether the analyst is giving the coffee out of his own need to be loved as a warm, giving, accepting figure, rather than paying primary attention to his role as a doctor and an analyst.

As I have said, Dr. Blanck makes some cogent points in her arguments, which cannot be dismissed casually on the basis of her being an "uptight lady." Although, since one of my arguments is that one must be authentic as an analyst, it makes sense that the way one analyst handles such a situation might not necessarily be the best way for all analysts to do so. My argument is that it is certainly true that the analyst must be aware of the exact place in his analysis the patient is at, and also whether the analyst does have a stake in presenting himself either generally or to that particular patient as a do-gooder and a better nurturer than the patient's mother. Furthermore, the analyst cannot overlook the latent content of the patient's request. Everything that happens between them is and must be grist for the analytic mill. If in his request, including the timing of it, the patient is indulging his dependency or avoiding either separation or rage at the analyst's withholding nurture, I can see the validity of refusing him. I

can also see the validity, even more so, if the patient charac-
terologically is a demanding person, who expects to be ser-
viced. On the other hand, if the analyst has quickly in his
mind sifted through all these possibilities and eliminated
them as important issues and sees the request on a simple
human level, then I see no reason for the withholding of the
coffee as long as the incident is analyzed if it appears to apply
to this patient's psyche at this moment in time.

I must say that most such requests I encounter do not
have the complicated psychoanalytic importance that Dr.
Blanck and others of her persuasion attribute to them.
These requests and their importance are also a function of
the milieu that is set up in the analytic situation. If an atmosphere of comfort and casual informality is set up by the
analyst, the request for coffee is not particularly inappropriate or noteworthy. If, on the other hand, an austere, cold,
"scientific" atmosphere is set up, then such a request might
have momentous significance. One contemporary analyst,
Dr. Robert Langs from Brooklyn, has written a book on
The Bi-Personal Field, in which his description of the analytic
milieu is almost like that of a sterile surgical field. I wrote a
paper chiding him by calling his book *The Bi-Impersonal
Field,* implying that what he omitted was the patient's—and
the analyst's—humanity.

In Harry Guntrip's last paper before his death, he con-
trasted his analysis with W. R. D. Fairbairn with his analysis
with Donald W. Winnicott. All three of these gentlemen are
important contributors to the English Object Relations
school. Fairbairn, however, was still very much under the
influence of classical analysis, used the couch, and was quite
austere and abstinent, whereas Winnicott was a much more
humanistic analyst. Guntrip recounts how Winnicott did in
fact frequently offer him a cup of coffee (or was it tea, since
they were English?). Winnicott believed that the analyst
should set up what he called a "holding environment," a
milieu in which the patient felt symbolically as if he were an
infant cradled in his mother's arms. This, he felt, created the

optimal situation for the patient to reveal his most hidden needs, wishes, and feelings. Guntrip felt that he derived a great deal more help from his analysis with Winnicott than he had from his previous analysis.

Of course, I tend to agree with Winnicott and Guntrip. However, interestingly enough, neither was very explicit about his actual behavior in the analytic situation. I am not clear, for instance, about their use of the couch. I tend to believe, since neither of them stated otherwise, that they continued to use it. I think in general that setting up an environment other than a "holding" one artificially introduces so many unnatural deprivations that the patient either conforms by hiding his feelings or rebels. This is not a matter of transference (inappropriate feelings from the past) but is a quite appropriate reaction to the present. If the analyst is in fact depriving and withholding, and sets up a cold, austere atmosphere, then the patient's anger at it is not therapeutic; it is a reasonable response to such ill-treatment. But, perhaps in this general area, we are again thrown back to the idea that there is more than one way to skin a cat. Dr. Langs, for example, in his books displays such arrogance and hostility in the way he deals with his supervisees that perhaps the patient is better off with him in his "bi-impersonal field" than with his authentic Self.

The important point is that there should be no standard universal manner in which all analysts present themselves. It should be a function of the analyst's person and his personality. When I was more austere as a person, I presented a more austere atmosphere to my patients. The crucial issue has to do with the analyst's authenticity. The material that comes up with one analyst may not come up with another. After all, we are dealing with a "bi-personal field." The analyst's trying to hide who he is is still a function of *who* he is, of that particular analyst's own psyche or theory. All that is analyzable here basically is the manner in which this particular patient reacts to this particular analyst. That is part of the reason that even Freud recommended continuing re-analysis for analysts at different periods in their lives. He did not add that this should occur with different analysts, but I think this recommendation has a great deal of merit. I often recommend and support a patient's going to another analyst after a period of time with me, perhaps to a woman if I think they have some issues that they have not been able to explore with me because of my gender. I also have been extremely permissive, even encouraging, of patients' involvements with other therapists or other forms of therapy concurrently with their seeing me. This certainly tends to mitigate any fears of my possessiveness of them and tends to encourage their emotional separation from me. So, many of my patients have used body therapy, Shiatsu therapy, EST, Actualizations, family therapy, couples therapy, been in group therapy with other therapists, or have even seen other individual analysts concurrent with seeing me for individual analysis. I also strongly recommend bibliotherapy—the patient's reading books in the field. All of the above are absolute anathema to classical analysts, who speak of "splitting the transference"—setting one therapist up as all good and the other as all bad—and voice other objections.

Are these objections valid, or are these analysts being possessive of their patients and insecure about losing them to someone else? I suppose again this depends upon the particular analyst in question. Dealing with these issues theoretically in detail would be too technical and beyond the aspirations of this book. But for me the generality still has to do with setting up a permissive "holding environment," in which the patient also has permission to wander and explore, as opposed to setting up a tight "bi-personal field," in which he does not.

We have wandered a bit afield from our practicing stage—I trust not inappropriately. To me, the analyst's encouragement of the patient's freedom to call him up for "refueling" during this stage in some ways transcends the issue of gratification versus abstinence. Yet the analysts who advocate abstinence would certainly not be free to take the position I advocate. They would not have such an option. My feeling is that I take this position not helter-skelter, nor because I like to be a giving person, nor even because I wish to emulate my father's dedication. Rather, I experience a dynamic understanding of the patient's position and the importance of my availability, especially at this time in his analysis, which makes it imperative for me to be available as an aid to his process of separation and individuation. If, in fact, the mother is not available for "refueling," the toddler is apt to become frightened, give up his efforts at venturing forth, and to return and regress toward a more symbiotic position with his mother. My "gratifying" him rather than "abstaining" promotes his separation from me rather than impedes it. In this sense, I feel my personality acts to help the patient at this particular juncture.

There may well be situations in which my personality impedes rather than encourages. I cannot just shrug this off and say, "Oh well, I've got to be me." I must try to understand the deficits in my personality and curb them to the best of my ability. If these deficits are parts of me that I cannot deal with without giving up my authenticity and presenting a false Self, then I must honestly discuss them with my patient as a way of letting him know he is brooking more with me on this particular issue than he might with another analyst. I am not very tolerant, for example, of guilt-producing complainers. My mother was one of these in a very subtle, covert way. If she had been more overt, I probably would have been able to be less negatively reactive to it. When I have a patient who exhibits these traits and I have negative reactions toward them, I explain to him that some of my overreactions come from my specific past.

But to continue with Dr. Mahler's theory, the next step after practicing is called by her "rapprochement." This is a very crucial stage in the development of autonomy. There is an almost equal and opposite pull between staying attached and venturing forth. The child, usually starting at about age two, goes out and has his adventures; yet he also wants to come back to his mother—not just for "refueling," but to share and discuss his activities. When a patient is in this sub-phase of separation, the analyst must listen patiently to much anecdotal material, which may not appear on the surface to be very analytic. Of course, if the analyst understands the point of development of his patient, he will recognize that the sharing and recounting of these anecdotes is an essential part of the patient's efforts at separation. I often involve myself in this process, not merely as a passive listener but much more as a participant, sharing some of my own experiences that appear to parallel the patient's. The opportunity for this kind of sharing and mutual discussion—very essential to the patient's progress—would also be precluded a priori by the classical analytic position.

Part of the subphase of rapprochement is termed by Dr. Mahler "the rapprochement crisis." At this point, the pull toward separateness and the equal pull backward toward symbiosis create a particularly difficult period of crisis for a patient. I think for a good many of us, this period may never be achieved until we go through what is now called a "midlife crisis." Dr. Mahler's early work suggested that this process of separation-individuation should hopefully be successfully completed by the age of three or four. In her latest book, she has revised her position. She now basically accepts the fact that most people continue to go through different examples of this crisis throughout their lives, achieving a greater and greater degree of separation in the process. That is the reason I feel midlife crisis is an adult version of the very issues Mahler describes in childhood. It certainly was so for me. Not until I had gone through my period of "death and resurrection" at thirty-seven and thirty-eight did I feel a relatively solid degree of autonomy. And, of course, I continue to experience mini-crises from time to time, during which I am pulled back toward merger with my partner and have an equally strong pull toward more independence and the ability to take steps that might be important for me while not pleasing my partner. (At the moment my writing this book is an example. We are on vacation together. Her preference would be for me to share the time with her. I have a strong pull to do so, both in order to please her and because time spent with her is very pleasurable for me. On the other hand, I have a strong urge to write this book and to express ideas which have been important to my being. Luckily for me, she is relatively understanding of this. However, even if she objected strongly, which she does on occasion, I would very likely persist in my writing, so risking her displeasure and the temporary rupture of our relationship.)

What, according to Mahler, is the pot of gold at the end of this rainbow? What is the stage to which we all aspire but which none of us really achieves? She calls this stage "object constancy." By this she does *not* mean that we stay with the same partner forever; rather, she means that we are able to internalize the person we have chosen to be with at this point in our lives, so that they are with us even when we are physically and/or emotionally separated from them. We are able to go through periods of mutual anger, different objectives, geographical separations, without losing the attachment we have with them. This is truly a wonderful position to which to aspire. Many interpersonal struggles would be less painful and less terrifying if both people had attained this level of connection.

Mahler's work focuses us on an aspect of child development that originally occurs before the Oedipus complex, though it continues throughout life. She puts us in touch with a theory that has clear and palpable meaning to us every day of our lives. She is not talking about esoteric theoretical physical science theories like the libido theory. She is talking about human beings and how lags or lapses in their early development have an impact on their daily lives. Overall, there has been a general acceptance of her work in the analytic community, but sometimes her ideas have been preempted and she has not received the credit for them that she deserves.

12

Kohut's Work on Narcissism

In the middle sixties I attended a convention of psychoanalysts in Buenos Aires and Rio de Janiero. Among my
traveling companions was a very quiet, mild, unobtrusive,
self-effacing man. I remember him as wearing gray and
being "gray"—so colorless was he. He said very little on the
trip and was always most pleasant. I had almost forgotten
this meeting until in 1971 he came out with a book that
changed the course of psychoanalysis in America. The man
was Dr. Heinz Kohut and the book was *The Analysis of the
Self.* It was extremely difficult; "written in Chinese," I liked
to say about it. When I read it, I became determined to
write the "English translation," and I finally did so in *Your
Own True Love,* which was published in 1975. I dedicated
the book to Dr. Kohut, "America's greatest living analyst."
Unfortunately, he died in 1982.

Until the appearance of Kohut's book, "narcissism" had
been a dirty word, not only in common parlance but also
within the analytic community. The literature on narcissism
had been extremely confusing. This confusion lay basically
in two different usages of the word. Semantics are so important, especially in psychoanalysis. Our basic tool for treatment is words. In any event, one meaning of "narcissism"
was healthy self-esteem. That had to be good; one could
not have too much of that. The other meaning of the word
was quite pejorative—an excessive preoccupation with one's
self. The latter was associated with a low self-esteem that
needed constant reinforcement. Since even in the analytic
literature the word had been used with both of these mean-

ings, the result was massive confusion. And within the current analytic community much of this confusion persists.

Kohut thinks of narcissism as a healthy linear process that goes from infantile archaic grandiosity to the development of healthy self-esteem. Dr. Otto Kernberg is the leader of the rival faction, which encompasses the American Psychoanalytic Association's position. His personality was almost the antithesis of Kohut's (as I had first met him). Kernberg is a rigid, arrogant, brusque middle-aged man, with a thick German accent, whose charm is in the same league with Henry Kissinger. Kernberg believes that narcissism is always a regressive defensive position, not a normal developmental process. That position is an infantile one, in which no one else's needs have any importance. We analysts used to joke that at analytic meetings half of the participants wore Kernberg T-shirts and the other half Kohut T-shirts. Kernberg, though a graduate of a South American Kleinian analytic institute, identified himself with the position of the American Psychoanalytic Association. Although there may be individual exceptions, most of these classical analysts basically disown Kohut's work.

Kohut described a somewhat unusual group of patients who, though they appeared very much intact and often functioned brilliantly, were nevertheless completely preoccupied with themselves and unable to make any sort of real attachment to another person. They were constantly striving for self-aggrandizement, were exhibitionistic, and extremely vulnerable to slights or narcissistic blows, which caused a sudden and decided drop in their self-esteem. He diagnosed these people as having "narcissistic character disorders."

In exploring the roots of their psychopathology, he discovered what he postulated to be the normal line of development of self-esteem. The infant starts out with the impression that he is the center of the universe. This is part of a normal period of megalomania and grandiosity that occurs during the first months of life. If he is fortunate, the infant will have a mother who beams at him and shares his view of himself that he is "the greatest." He will perceive the gleam in his mother's eye and be reassured of his own importance. Also his every wish will become his mother's command. After he has had his share of this situation and his mother has had her share of it as well, time and the exigencies of life will force the mother to pay attention to other issues—other children, her husband, her work—and gradually to wean our precious Christ-child from his throne atop the universe.

Once again, from a third source—Object Relations and Mahler being the first two—we have a focus on first-year-of-life experience and the mother–child dyad. If the mother for whatever reason is not available to provide this gleam, the child will be left unfulfilled. He will be destined to provide this constant attention to himself, or compulsively and hopelessly he will try to find someone to provide it for him. He will be addicted to getting attention. This will make him basically unable to care seriously about anyone's welfare but his own. He will have a low self-esteem and be self-centered. The battle is not totally lost if the mother does not come through. If he is fortunate, he may be able to idealize parts of his father or others, introject them (take them into himself as part of himself), and achieve a degree of self-esteem in admiring those things in himself that he previously admired in his father or others.

If he has a nongleaming mother and an unidealizable father and no other person of note replaces his father, then the poor fellow may, like Narcissus, spend the rest of his days metaphorically looking at his own reflection and gleaming upon himself. But over the years, like Narcissus, he will wither away emotionally, ending up a lonely, empty, depleted person. As he grows older and less attractive and his powers in various areas begin to fail, he will compulsively be attempting with diminishing success to maintain his self-esteem. His more frequent failures will make him angry, bitter, despondent, and ultimately full of self-hatred. Since he has been unable to establish close relationships, he will not successfully be able to lean on others for the support he needs. So the myth about Narcissus is a quite accurate metaphor for his withering away and dying emotionally.

Kohut's idea of treating this kind of patient was for the analyst to set himself up as an empathic figure. He felt the problem had to do with a developmental gap rather than a conflict between instinct, conscience, and external reality (id, superego, and ego). This gap could only be remedied by the analyst's providing, within certain clear limits, what the mother had not been able to in his infancy nor the father or father-surrogate later on. So Kohut's stance was one of empathy and understanding without much interpretation. These people were so vulnerable that even a rather innocuous interpretation might be experienced by them as a narcissistic blow. Kohut described a series of transferences that occurred regularly in therapy with these patients, which finally allowed them to increase their self-esteem. This in turn would help them to relate to others in a more caring manner.

In fact, the particular group of patients that fits Kohut's category exactly is rather rare; I doubt that I have seen more than five or six of them in over thirty-five years of practice. However, in opening up the whole subject of narcissism, Kohut enlightened us about many issues from which all of us suffer to a greater or lesser degree. To the degree that most of us have been deprived of either the maternal or paternal ways of increasing our self-esteem, we all have fears of our reverting back to a grandiose archaic Self. We are frightened of two major consequences: the megalomania which, uncontrolled, could easily be destructive to others or render us psychotic; and the humiliation which would be our fate once the grandiosity was discovered. So most of us defend ourselves against this grandiosity.

One major mechanism of defense is self-effacement. Remember Kohut's personality in the sixties—he was a classic example of this. Often, an analyst writes about what he knows best, his own psychopathology. (Since mine is multifaceted, I have been able to write on many subjects!) An individual as self-effacing as Kohut was thinks little of himself, hides his sterling qualities, and disappears into a corner. He suffers from a lack of self-esteem. The other kind of defense against our fears of grandiosity is not to take in any positive attention we get, despite having a compulsive need to elicit it. People of this type are far from self-effacing. They are exhibitionistic and constantly getting attention, sometimes of a not altogether positive type, since they can be annoying. But the positive attention they get runs like water through a sieve. They are unable to internalize any of it, so they are constantly seeking to replace it. Most of us have one or the other set of defenses against our fears of grandiosity.

My form of treatment for these problems is to try to make these fears and the grandiosity behind them conscious. Then they can be looked at with amusement rather than panic and the defenses they call forth can be mitigated. Of course, in trying to provide a "holding environment," I like to think that I am automatically supplying for all of my patients a substitute for the empathic mother who makes the patient the center of her universe. Once again analytic therapy becomes an attempt to repair *within the doctor–patient dyad* what was lacking in the original mother–child dyad. And where else in the world but in the analytic situation can a person command the total attention of another person whose complete focus is on him? The answer is clearly nowhere. As a matter of fact, there is strong speculation, certainly among Kohut and his followers, but among others as well, that this is the therapeutic agent in any psychoanalytic system. What is the constant that makes patients well in any system? The relationship with the therapist. Why did my patients get well thirty years ago when I was using inadequate and even "wrong" Freudian theory and technique? Why do they seem to have responded to whatever theory was in vogue with me throughout the years? The constant was my commitment to an attention that was riveted on them.

In fact, however, I do not really believe this replay of the past that was lacking in the mother–child dyad is the *only* curative agent, as do Kohut's followers. But I believe it is an important factor. I feel strongly, as I have said, that cognition—intellectual understanding of the problem—by the patient plays a very important role. (This is where understanding of theory by the analyst comes in.) I also feel that the old Pavlovian deconditioning plays an important role. Another part of the change certainly occurs through the internalization of certain idealized or even real parts of the analyst. How did I learn to care about people when almost everyone in my childhood environment was so totally uncaring about me? I have no doubt that the major factor in this was my internalization of my thirteen analysts. With the possible exception of my training analyst, the others—despite their theoretical and personal inadequacies—were certainly listening to me, focused on trying to help me, trying in whatever misguided way to relieve my pain. Where else in the world, I repeat, can a person find another human being who is so altruistic, even for forty-five minutes a week?

Some theorists also put a great deal of stock in the suggestive power of analysis. They feel that if a patient and an analyst share in the belief that the analyst knows what he or she is doing and can help, then the person will be helped. African witch-doctors, who used to be disparaged, are now being studied very seriously. Since such a high percentage of our illnesses have a large psychosomatic component, perhaps this factor made witch doctors nearly as effective as some of our modern physicians and analysts. Charismatic analysts with a strong sense of belief in themselves often have better results with patients than self-effacing ones. Immodestly, I would have to include myself in this category. I do think this element of suggestion plays a role in achieving good results.

Classical psychoanalysts are likely to say and, in fact, have said personally to me that they think Kohut's analytic stance is nothing more than glorified babysitting. They naturally see his position as the ultimate in gratification of a patient and the lack of proper abstinence. In truth, Kohut does not gratify the patient. He gives him empathic, understanding interpretations, but nothing more. Kernberg, the villain wearing the black hat, believes that narcissism should always be attacked as a regressive defense. A defense against what? Well, of course, the Oedipus complex. This response to the issue of narcissism puts into perspective, in my opinion, the obtuseness and rigidity of classical analysts. They dismiss what to many others has seemed to be a major advance in psychoanalytic theory. I have supervised some therapists who treated narcissistic character disorders. Although I have not treated any such disorders myself, I have treated many patients with important narcissistic components in their makeup, and my own experience strongly corroborates Kohut's. These patients, until their narcissistic wounds are at least partially repaired, respond to any interpretation as an assault. Kohut in his second book, *The Restoration of the Self,* speculates on the possibility that all that we call negative transference may in truth be an appropriate response on the part of the patient to empathic failures of the analyst. I have had my share of empathic failures; they certainly can and do produce this appropriate reaction of rage in a patient. On the other hand, I think Kohut goes a little too far in his speculation. In my opinion, not all negative transferences result from empathic failures.

This leads me to the unhappy tale of my last encounter with what I expected to be the same, meek, self-effacing Dr. Kohut. It was in 1978 in Chicago, his bailiwick, at the First International Conference on the Psychology of the Self. I was pleased to be one of the invited speakers. In 1978 I was among a handful of Kohut's admirers in New York, but what I experienced at the conference appalled me. This was not a scientific meeting but a testimonial to Kohut. He had dropped his self-effacing defense and become—naturally—quite grandiose. He had a whole coterie of "groupies" surrounding him. They were saying that *all* patients should be treated by his technique, that in effect practically everything else ever written in the field of psychoanalysis was now obsolete.

At a dinner for the speakers I sat next to a woman who had written one of the most thoughtful, brilliant papers I had ever read in an ego-psychological vein, following the theories of Dr. Mahler. When I complimented her on her paper, she totally dismissed it, saying it was misguided. There was now one and only one truth and that was the WORD handed down by the prophet. Or was he more than a prophet? An analyst from Los Angeles and myself presented papers praising Kohut for making a contribution to the field and showing some of the interconnections between his work and that of Mahler and the Object Relations analysts. Our papers were very coolly received and argued against by Kohut's groupies. I saw the same old story unfolding that I had seen so many times before in my career. A person makes a significant contribution to the field. He and his followers, in making legitimate changes in existing theories, then proceed to throw out the baby with the bath water. Mahler's contributions were totally dismissed. Is there not an obvious connection between her symbiotic phase and Kohut's period of perfect union between mother and child? Of course not, they said. The most amusing and saddening twist was the manner in which Kohut in many ways proved his own thesis. Instead of going from self-effacing to grandiose to a normal level of self-esteem, he became stuck in the grandiosity. And now I had also lost my idealized father!

The situation of an adult getting stuck in grandiosity has happened to too many men who within their subculture have achieved almost unlimited power. Hitler, Mussolini, Nixon, Idi Amin, Pol Pot are all examples of this within my lifetime. This grandiosity invariably gets out of hand and leads to the demise of the leader. Democracy has safeguards against it, but Nixon, at least for a while, managed to evade them. One of the reasons for the numerous controversies in psychoanalysis is that there have been so many individuals who contributed enormously, but then lost their perspective and could brook no opposition. Freud was certainly one of these; he could not remain in the same organization as Jung or Adler. And Freudians—obviously among others—have continued his exclusionary tactics. I have always had the dream of trying to put together the contributions made by different theorists into one whole frame; several of my papers have tried to address this issue. This book is a partial attempt at the task.

13

Melanie Klein

In my early days of psychoanalysis, I read the works of Melanie Klein. She was almost completely disparaged in those days as a woman who postulated some fanciful reconstructions about what went on in the minds of infants. I was discouraged from pursuing my interest in her and in truth I myself did not then find her theories especially cogent or applicable. Thirty years later—in the late seventies—I rediscovered her work. I now believe her to be the most profound analytic thinker of our age. Perhaps I have found yet another guru, who will be displaced; perhaps I have found another parental archetype who will disappoint me. But I like to think this is not the case. After all, her work has been around for more than fifty years, and most English and Central and South American analysts follow her lead more than Freud's.

Klein herself started out very much within the Freudian framework. However, she specialized in the psychoanalyses of children—even very young ones, three and four years old. Once again we are brought back to the concept of child observation, which led to Mahler's and Bowlby's conclusions. Klein did her level best to stay within the Freudian camp; in some of her work she even stretches credibility a bit, such as trying to show that six-month-old babies have Oedipal problems. However, her focus is almost exclusively on the mother–child dyad and the complicated interactions that occur within it. Much of this material is rather difficult for the layman; indeed, it is quite difficult for a seasoned professional. I have read what is perhaps her most famous essay, "Envy and Gratitude," at least five times. Each time I learn some important point that had eluded me previously. I shall not attempt to give anything but the most cursory summary of her theories here because of their difficulty.

In brief, she postulates that all infants are born with a natural predisposition to be destructive; their rage is not *only* reactive to deprivation or other wrongs. Kohut, for example, believed that man is not innately destructive. One of the most controversial points in Freud's work is on this issue. He is in agreement with Klein—or rather, Klein was in agreement with him. Even some of the most classical analysts parted company with Freud on this particular point. I feel it is more than a philosophical speculation, because it colors our total view of man, and has tremendous implications for his existence as a social animal—as well as what we can expect to do for him in therapy.

Despite a recent tendency among anthropologists to minimize their work, my beliefs follow those of Robert Ardrey in his excellent book *African Genesis,* and other anthropologists such as the Leakeys, that man is descended from predatory apes. Even if this is not true anthropologically, it is certainly in man's nature to be destructive. Anyone who has lived through the last fifty years as spectator to the Holocaust, Hiroshima, Vietnam, and Cambodia and who continues to dispute this shows, to my mind, an incredible naivete. Of course, politically the belief that man is aggressive has important implications. It makes pacifism appear to be totally ridiculous. It assumes that men will continue to destroy unless there are enormous penalties built in to curb this. We are back once more to Pavlov. If we can institute a system in which aggression is punished severely, perhaps we can control it. We can never expect to extinguish it.

The translation of these ideas into the daily practice of a psychoanalyst is quite important. We cannot expect to produce peace-loving patients who have no primitive destructiveness. We can help people to accept these feelings in themselves and convert them into more effective assertive ones, but they will not and do not evaporate or disappear, even when many of them have been channeled into more constructive areas. Kohut, who disagreed with Klein, felt that all of man's destructive rage was a reaction to empathic failures in his environment. This distinction may sound philosophical rather than of practical importance. But, in fact, it has direct implications for psychoanalysis. When Kohut—following this theory—ends up by saying that all rage in a patient is reactive to empathic failures on the part of the analyst, and that the patient does not bring his own baggage or rage into the office, then we have a very practical difference in approach. Kohut in his second book virtually dismisses negative transference—the projection of old angers onto the analyst. He considers the patient's rage as being a reaction to empathic failures on the part of the mother in infancy, and later of the analyst. This dismisses the patient's constitutional destructive tendencies.

I believe that one reason why Klein has been and even now continues to be disparaged in America is because of her insistence that the child comes into the world—and the patient comes into analysis—with an inborn destructive tendency. She elaborates a complicated system of the course of these destructive feelings, much of which arose from her work with very young children. The child is born with the tendency to be enraged at the mother's power to give and withhold the breast. He is so envious of this power that he is apt to wish to destroy the mother even when she is not withholding the breast. He literally wishes to bite the hand (or breast) that feeds him. He also projects his own primitive rage onto and into the mother and is then terrified that it may be directed back against himself. Horror movies are an example of these projected monsters; these movies have large audiences today. They resonate with some of our primitive inborn fears. But we must remember that such monsters are no one but ourselves. In the Bronx Zoo there is a cage with the heading: "The most destructive animal in

150

the world." When you look directly into the cage, you see yourself in a mirror.

Human history has certainly shown that no species of animal is as destructive as man to his own species, and our current history gives sad testimony to this. I believe that an acceptance and understanding of these primitive destructive parts of ourselves is essential to any attempt at mental health. Klein confronts the monsters and attempts to tame them. On the other hand, she certainly does not hold the equally extreme belief, that man is all bad. In fact, she describes the process through which some of our primitive rage can be directed toward love. She feels that if we confront our primitive destructiveness head on, we will feel guilty about our wish to destroy the very person who feeds us and comforts us. In contrast, we may not feel too guilty about wanting to retaliate against a person who has hurt us. However, this primitive rage is senseless destruction when it means biting the hand that feeds you, and such rage can have no redeeming features.

If we acknowledge our rage toward those who nurture us and our guilt about it, then we will be prompted to make reparations to them. The end point of this process is gratitude for what we receive rather than envy of the person's power to withhold. This gratitude, Klein feels, is the beginning of being able to feel genuine love and caring for another person. Her views can hardly be labeled as cynical. Love, in fact, is born of hate.

Freud postulated that there is no guilt in a human being until the Oedipus complex. A person feels guilty about wanting to eliminate the parent of the same sex merely as a convenience to his having access to the parent of the opposite sex. Oedipal guilt is a reaction toward destructiveness that is not retaliatory to some injury but in the service of increased sexual pleasure. Klein in working with young children found that there was a guilt that appeared in the first year of life that was also connected to a destructiveness that was not retaliatory but inborn.

Direct observation of children by Klein, Mahler, and Bowlby among others required, even demanded a change in theory. Yet many classical analysts continue to maintain their blindness, as in "The Emperor's New Clothes," to all these discoveries. In order to maintain their dogma, their illusion of Freud's infallibility, and their adherence to the Word, they blithely discount new and even old discoveries (Klein was writing as early as the 1930s). In addition, Americans seem to have a tendency toward naivete, toward looking at the world through rose-colored glasses. Just as Freud's discoveries of childhood sexuality appalled the Viennese in the 1890s, these discoveries of the autocratic, grandiose, destructive aspects of "innocent little babies" appall many of us now. So there has been a general tendency toward disowning these parts of ourselves, and especially a tendency against labeling them as innate or constitutional. Our religions tell us that man was created in the perfect image of God. What would these theories do to that concept!

I believe it is these factors that have tended to keep many if not most American psychoanalysts in a classical Freudian mold. Interestingly enough, they have to do with idealization of Freud's as well as the baby's perfection. Klein feels that idealization is one of the major defenses against our primitive rage and envy. If we put someone so far above us, we cannot ever allow ourselves to envy and hate them for their power, beauty, wealth, or other attributes of theirs we would want to posses. The manner in which this process occurs in analysis is obvious. The analyst is idealized. The analyst and patient in classical analysis have an unspoken agreement not to disturb this idealization. The classical analytic stance supports the persistence of the idealization, since it is never attacked by the analyst. While this persists, neither the analyst nor the patient has to soil himself with these nasty primitive emotions of rage and envy.

The only way to get the patient in touch with his primitive rage is for the analyst to make a consistent assault on this idealization. In my early days of group therapy, I did this by presenting myself with all my foibles. This certainly succeeded in evoking a great deal of primitive rage. Now that I have a much more solid theoretical base since my rediscovery of Klein, I attack the idealization with a more direct frontal approach as well. This is almost invariably followed by the sequence of primitive rage, guilt, reparation, gratitude, and love.

Idealization is not the only defense against this primitive rage. Other defenses include devaluing the envied person (for his power or whatever else) and devaluing the Self. The latter is a terribly painful symptom. A person who envies an attribute, possession, or quality of someone else he admires and who cannot bear the guilt for these base feelings may turn his primitive rage against himself. "Who am I, a worm, to envy that prince? I am so low I cannot ever even aspire in my wildest dreams to be what he is." These devastating attacks on the Self are among the most painful episodes I have seen in my practice. Ruth was a good example of this problem.

Ruth's *real* objective life could hardly be faulted. Now in her late forties, she had been married for almost thirty years to a very bright, talented, successful man who loved her dearly. In fact almost all of her acquaintances admired her and were very fond of her. She was clever, warm, attractive, and extremely gracious. After her children had grown up, she pursued a career and was very successful at it. She had a wonderful sense of humor and the ability to be playful and to enjoy athletic, cultural, and social occasions. Why was Ruth a patient? Her life was really enviable. Ah, but that was the problem—many people did envy her. And each time she was aware of someone's envy, she defended against her fear of their fantasied envious attacks on her by devaluing herself in the most devastating way. She, in her mind, made herself and her life a total disaster and suffered terribly, feeling she was the most unfortunate woman in the world.

Why should she have these terrible self-destructive reactions to someone's envy of her? Well, there was another kind of situation that would also produce this reaction. If Ruth was at a party and ran into a woman whom she perceived as being more attractive than she, Ruth would begin to experience herself as the ugliest woman in the world. She defended herself against her envy of the more beautiful woman by devaluing herself. But at times she could feel her envious rage at the more beautiful woman—her conscious destructive wish to destroy her "rival" and take her beauty away from her.

This process could explain her fear of other people's envy of her. In effect, she projected the degree of her own envy onto the person who envied her. As I told her, she thought that others were as rotten and vicious as she was. No wonder she feared their envious rage.

Now where did all of this come from? Ruth's mother and three sisters were all extremely envious. It must have run in the family. Ruth was born with the same genes as her mother and sisters. But beyond this, her mother and sister would viciously attack and destroy one another, and Ruth too, if anyone had any success in life. Even now her sisters continue to attack her when they become aware of some triumph or some fortunate occurrence in her life. Ruth's envy, both her own and her projected envy, were ruining what could have been an extremely happy life.

After we had carefully exposed all these psychodynamics, I began to try to encourage Ruth to understand how these issues were played out in her relationship to me. Oh, she had absolutely no envy of me. How was it covered up? Initially, she idealized me as the "greatest" in my field—a position beyond her aspirations. Since she was also a psychotherapist and not as successful as I, how come she didn't envy me? When I began to chip away at her idealization of me, she noticed that she started to go into one of her terrible self-devaluating depressions before each of our sessions. So her next defense was to devalue herself. When this defense was understood, she began to devalue me and my treatment of her. She was wasting her time; I was not really helping her; she was feeling worse than when she had started with me. When this defense was also understood, her primitive envy of me began to emerge. She attacked me, was furious at me, had dreams of mangling me. Her envy of me had now become conscious. This phase of treatment was followed by a period in which she felt very guilty about her meanness toward me (simultaneously she was having similar reactions at home to her husband). She felt truly guilty and made reparations by apologizing and being grateful for my patience and for the help I had given her. After going through this cycle several times with me in therapy, her symptoms began to abate both in frequency and in severity.

The "cure" came from a combination of insight (cognition) into the process and the patient's awareness of her rage toward me. As long as I had allowed the idealization of myself to persist, none of these things could ever have happened. The analysis of the really deep material would have been left untouched, and—more than that—covered over by destructive defenses.

I do not believe everyone's major problem has to do with primitive envious rage. I think perhaps 10 percent of my patients have that as their major issue. However, the feelings are present to a degree in all patients. A thorough awareness of the dynamics is essential to the patient, in my judgment.

There are some strong parallels between Kohut and Klein, despite their basic theoretical differences about the presence of destructive rage at birth. Kohut talks about the defense against archaic destructive grandiosity through self-effacement. This does not differ too much from Klein's defense against primitive rage through devaluing the Self. Klein also asserts that the presence of good mothering mitigates the rage and helps the infant to move forward through the cycle of guilt, reparation, gratitude, and love. Kohut feels that having the gleam from mother's or the analyst's eye helps transform primitive archaic grandiosity into healthy self-esteem.

Klein certainly did not get her ideas from Kohut; she antedated him by many years. Kohut, on the other hand, must have been familiar with Klein's material. I am obviously not suggesting he plagiarized her ideas. Yet when it was suggested to him that his theories did not suddenly spring from his head as Athena did from the head of Zeus, he took offense at this as an assault on him. If only analysts could think of contributions to a general body of knowledge, rather than each one feeling either himself or his particular chosen guru to be the sole possessor of the Truth! For me, all of the analysts I have mentioned—Freud, Reich, Klein, Kohut, Guntrip, and the others—as well as many I have not mentioned, have made important contributions to the body of knowledge I use daily. And I am still seeking new contributors.

14

How Do I Practice?

I have a newsletter in front of me from one of the analytic societies to which I belong. In it there is a column called "The Inquiring Reporter." The question asked of the analysts is: "What professional issues would you most like to hear comments on by your colleagues?" And the first answer is: "I would like to know more about how people really work in the privacy of their offices." Other questions have included: How do analysts deal with specific life events such as death in their families? What defenses are employed in their work with patients? When life events are pressing, how do these events affect analytic work? How does one deal with isolation and the absence of peer feedback? How does the analyst's need for a vacation impinge on the psychic life of the patient? How many patients are seen in a week and how frequently do they come each week? What is the average length of treatment of these patients? How does one's work and practice change over the course of one's professional life? How are expectations of financial reward consonant and/or dissonant with the philosophy of psychoanalysis?

One analyst comments: "Many analysts believe that the patient is free to leave treatment at any time and voice this option to the patient. Some present-day analysts appear to believe that they have a contract with the patient which requires mutual agreement for termination. How do these two points of view affect the patient's autonomy?" And another asks: "How do analysts actually handle the classical analytic tools—the couch, anonymity, abstinence? Do they combine analysis with other therapies—group therapy, dance or Yoga, biofeedback, etc.?"

One of the reasons for this plethora of questions by analysts is that there has been a great deal of secrecy and obfuscation about what they actually do within the privacy of their offices. This trend began with Freud himself, who apparently broke every rule of technique he himself laid down as dogma. Evidently he was much less formal and much more humanly responsive to his patients than he admitted in his writing. Patients of his have written books describing their analytic experience with him as being very different from what he advocated in theory. He was trying hard to make psychoanalysis a science, so he deliberately hid some of his own human responses to his patients, both good ones and bad ones. And, since Freud, this trend has continued among psychoanalysts. They have been ashamed to reveal themselves and to open for public examination what they really do with a patient. Analytic societies have handed down rigid rules of behavior, especially on such issues as the use of the couch, abstinence, anonymity, fees, and vacations, all of which are ways to eliminate the factor of the analyst's humanity and uniqueness.

Analysts have become afraid to reveal their humanity or any of the details of their interpersonal interactions with a patient for fear they will be drummed out of the corps and not considered by their colleagues to be honest-to-goodness "Kosher" psychoanalysts. They have devised a term, "psychoanalytically oriented psychotherapy," to describe a treatment based on analytic ideas but not adhering to the rigorous standards of analysis. This gives them an out. They must, perforce, accept the concept that there are other kinds of psychotherapy that can be helpful: after all, only one out of ten psychiatrists in America has completed formal analytic training. So they themselves are free to do therapy that does not adhere to the rigid standards. Therefore when they treat a patient who comes less than four times a week, who does not use the couch, who is treated in a more flexible, human manner, they simply say that this patient is not in analysis—he is receiving psychoanalytically oriented psychotherapy. I wish I had a penny for every word that has been written attempting to distinguish the difference between psychoanalytically oriented psychotherapy and pure analysis. For years analysts have been using this ruse in attempting to maintain their own purity while in fact violating it with the vast majority of their patients.

Very few, if any, analysts have many patients that they see four or five times a week using the couch and adhering to the rules of abstinence and anonymity. What patient, except a multimillionaire, could begin to be able to afford such treatment? Analytic candidates whose training requires them to have two or three such patients have a difficult time finding them. And almost every analytic candidate I have known has confessed to me that he has lied to his supervising control analyst about what he actually did and said with his patients; he was correctly and appropriately afraid that he would be punished or thrown out.

So the myths continue to be perpetuated about what analysts do with their patients. My first book, *Voyage from Lesbos,* was a session-by-session report of what transpired between myself and my patient in the course of a five-year analysis. I was surprised at that time in the late fifties that there were practically no other case reports on what actually went on in the treatment of a patient. There were volumes and volumes about theory, metapsychology, theories of technique; but no analyst had actually reported the course of an analysis. Of course Freud had written case reports about his treatment of some patients—Dora, Anna O., The Wolf-Man, Little Hans—around the turn of the century. But when he became discouraged about the inaccuracy of the childhood experiences his patients reported, he turned to the libido theory, and his subsequent writing became largely metapsychological (about theory) rather than clinical. So what really went on in the privacy of the consultation room became almost totally irrelevant in the psychoanalytic literature. The real transactions between two human beings—patient and analyst—were lost in the mountain of theory. This is quite incredible!

In any event, the classical analysts dodge the issue of what they do in actual practice by saying: "I have two analytic patients. The rest of my practice consists of patients in psychoanalytic psychotherapy." In the latter category they are allowed to break all the rigorous rules of psychoanalytic technique. But, in fact, since perhaps only one-tenth of the patients that most classical analysts treat are by *their* definition in analysis, what we have is the perpetuation of a myth. The analysts who might look kindly on my work might say: "Oh, he's a very skillful psychoanalytic psychotherapist, but he doesn't practice psychoanalysis." Within their parameters and their definition, I do not. But in fact *neither do they,* with rare exceptions.

Once again we are dealing with a case of "The Emperor's New Clothes," in which there is a mutual agreement to be blind about an obvious reality. Of course, all these analysts go around feeling guilty and fraudulent because they know they do not practice what they preach. And there is such a conspiracy of silence maintained that analysts have to ask the questions quoted at the beginning of this chapter. They want to know what other analysts actually do in their transactions with patients. Are they the only analysts who are culprits and frauds? They are afraid to reveal what occurs in their own practice for fear of losing their status as "psychoanalysts" and being labeled with the disparaging and pejorative term of being "merely psychoanalytic psychotherapists." The former term used to be connected exclusively with M.D.s while the latter was relegated to psychologists and social workers. This stratification through the type of academic degree continues to have a strong impact in the field, despite the fact that Freud himself wrote a work called *The Question of Lay Analysis* in which he strongly advocated dropping the medical training as part of analytic requirements.

My definition of a psychoanalyst is a person who has successfully completed analytic training in an "accredited" analytic institute. The issue of what is "accredited" becomes a problem. If "accredited" means accepted by the major analytic societies in America, all nonmedical analysts are automatically ruled out, despite their many major contributions to the field. I would include many analytic schools that have established reputations and reasonable credentials for analytic training. In fact, I myself have been on the faculty of several of these schools. I can attest to the excellence of their training and can compare it favorably to my own training and that provided by the so-called accredited analytic institutes. Since my definition includes all those who have completed this training, it is not limited by what these analysts do with their patients—how many times a week they are seen, whether they use the couch, whether they adhere to the rules of abstinence, anonymity, and so on. It seems to me that any other definition of the psychoanalyst is a great deal of double talk that is used to maintain an elitist structure.

So, after all this "preamble," let us come to the "constitution." What do I really do in the privacy of *my* office? Let me try to be as honest as I can be in revealing these deep dark secrets and breaking the "gentleman's agreement" with my colleagues to keep pretending I follow the rules. My office is in New York City on 78th Street off Madison Avenue. It is on the second floor of a converted townhouse. I have a large inner office which is carefully soundproofed with a double door; a foyer; a small waiting room; a bathroom; and a small kitchen, which is closed off. I work five days a week. I usually start about 8 A.M. and finish on the average about 7 P.M. I take a half-hour or forty-five minutes for lunch. My individual sessions last forty-five minutes. I rarely have any break between patients. I am

161

very punctual. I have three group therapy sessions a week, each of which runs for one and a half hours, and I do a few hours of supervision during which I review the cases of other analysts. At this time I no longer teach classes in analytic institutes, but I do give two marathons a year to candidates at one of the analytic institutes. These marathons are extended group therapy sessions in which I attempt to help a group of people who are strangers to me to get in touch with some of their repressed feelings. My fees for individual analysis and for supervision are seventy-five dollars per session; those for groups twenty-five dollars per session. The groups usually have from six to ten patients in them.

Most of my patients see me once a week; some are conjointly in group therapy once a week. I see a few patients twice a week, but none more frequently than this. The average patient of mine is in treatment for about four years. Sometimes I take patients at lower fees or continue to see them without fee when they run into financial reverses. I usually bill people at the end of the month and rarely have difficulty collecting fees, though I have had difficulties in the past on occasion. I am very flexible about waiting to be paid if the patient for one reason or another does not have the money available at the time of the bill. Sometimes I have allowed patients to accumulate debts of thousands of dollars but this has rarely led to my not getting paid. Usually there is a relationship of trust in this area. I am also very flexible about allowing patients to cancel appointments in advance and to change their time without charge when exigencies occur in their lives. I do not believe that my time and my schedule are necessarily more important than my patients'. I always try to accommodate their needs for changes and can usually do so.

I strongly deplore the usual analytic practice of charging a patient for his session if he is unable to make it; the only time I do this is if the patient does not let me know that he is not coming. Even then I may not charge if it is a rare occurrence that might have been based on a misunderstanding or a rare incident of forgetting. I treat some businessmen who have heavy traveling schedules and cannot be in New York at the same time every week. I think my fees are about the lowest in town for an analyst with my experience. I am shocked and unhappy about young analysts or even older analysts charging one hundred and fifty dollars a session and up—I have even heard that some charge as much as three or four hundred dollars. I do not believe that charging a patient for services is incompatible with treating him; however, I do feel that a person who becomes an analyst should not have accumulation of wealth as one of his goals. If that in fact is an important goal, he will be better off in finance or some medical surgical specialty, or more recently in law. Some lawyers charge $150 to $250 an hour and more; that is their prerogative, but I do not think they have the same relationship of trust and intimacy that I have with my patients.

Financial exploitation of a patient or an exorbitant fee follows the culture of greed in our country and creates a situation that can be inimical to the analytic process. An analyst should be paid a modest fee for his services that enables him to enjoy a comfortable lifestyle. My patients practically never complain about my fees, even when I have raised them. They are aware of the average fees for services and know very well that mine are at the bottom of the spectrum. I do not feel I am being masochistic about this. Rather, I believe low fees help create a "holding environment" in which a patient feels comfortable and cared for, and does not constantly have to lower his lifestyle in order to afford the fee. Of course, there are patients who cannot afford my fee even with the help of insurance. Sometimes, if I feel strongly that I have a particular affinity for the patient and will enjoy working with him, I will take him on at a reduced fee; often I will refer him to one of my colleagues, usually not an M.D., who charges less than I do.

I think analysts do a great deal of double talking when it comes to fees. Many or even most charge a patient whether or not he comes—even if he is on vacation or an extended business trip. I have even on occasion heard of an analyst who charges when *he* is on vacation. How analysts rationalize any of these procedures is beyond me. To me, all of them are clearly for the convenience and financial security of the analyst. They create a superior-inferior exploitive relationship, which I believe is counterproductive to good therapy. How can an analyst help a patient to become assertive and independent, and not to be masochistic, when the very acceptance of this kind of analytic situation conditions the patient to be the opposite?

What about the old joke about the young analyst who asks the older analyst: "How can you keep from getting tired and bored listening to your patients all week long?" The older analyst replies: "Who listens?" Is it true? Do I listen? Does it get boring? I can answer honestly that I always listen—yes, every moment. And the listening is of much greater intensity than when I listen to my wife or to television. Patients are amazed that I can recall the most insignificant details that came up years before in their analysis. I remember on one occasion a patient of mine said, "I'm sure you couldn't remember, but I had a dream three years ago in which I went into a diner for breakfast, ordered Post Toasties, and then . . ." I interrupted him. "It wasn't Post Toasties," I said, "it was Wheaties." He nearly fell out of the chair. When he asked how I could possibly remember such a detail, I explained to him that it depended on my concentration and on my needing to put all the material he presented into a sort of giant computer. So some insignificant detail crept in along with more significant material. I might not remember what *I* had had for breakfast that morning, because it was not stored up in any special memory bank.

We analysts do listen. And I think the position of two chairs facing one another at an angle rather than sitting behind a couch greatly facilitates this. I can remember my mind wandering while I was sitting behind the couch. Then I was observing the patient. Now the patient and I are communicating with one another. The latter is a situation of intensity that compels concentration and aliveness. If I begin to feel bored and to drift into some reverie or obsession, that is a signal that the patient is resisting or that I have a counterresistance to what the patient is saying. I check myself and the patient out in order not to allow the boredom and lack of communication to continue. Usually I can figure out what the trouble is and correct it. Sometimes I enlist the patient's help in breaking this stalemate. As I have stated, I am fortunate to be able to choose patients with whom I feel a rapport and with whom I can communicate easily. This undoubtedly is an enormous aid to my work. Rarely, two or three times a year, a patient and I have what is called a "golden hour." This is a session in which he and I have almost "perfect pitch" for one another's unconscious. These sessions are remarkably exhilarating experiences. However, even in normal sessions this kind of intensity for such long hours is depleting. People I have lived with have often complained that, in truth, "I gave at the office" and had little left when I got home. One way I have tried to remedy this is by taking a good deal of time off. I usually take six to eight weeks off in the summer, ten days at Christmas, and ten more at Easter. One of the questions asked by the analysts at the beginning of the chapter was about the impact of these vacations on the patient. None of the patients I see have any significant crises in their lives that they are unable to handle. They come to analysis to grow as people rather than to receive support or advice. This is not to say that I never give support or advice to a patient. And this, of course, counters another analytic dictum. As I have said, when a patient is in the process of separation-individuation, for example, I encourage his moves in the direction of autonomy and strongly encourage his taking courageous, anxiety-laden paths rather than the safe ones. But, overall, my patients are mature adults who are not dependent on me. So for most of them most of the time, my vacations do not pose much of a problem. The child in them may resent being abandoned, but the adult can handle the situation.

Exceptions are those patients who after great effort have broken through their defenses against intimacy and contacted their needy baby. Unfortunately, as happens occasionally when these feelings have come into consciousness shortly before my vacations, they may experience the rage, depression, and apathy that an infant does when he is left by his mother. I would prefer for the patient's sake *not* to leave at that time. If a patient is opening up right before a long break, I may attempt to do what I can to retard the process of his opening up until I return. However, at times this is not possible. My patient and I regret the pain he has had to experience, but the adult part of both of us realizes that without my vacations, I would not be much good for very long for any of my patients. I have to be aware of my own emotional needs and my own limitations. If I stretch my working beyond certain limits, I know from experience that the quality diminishes as I experience "burn-out."

This raises another question that was asked by the analysts at the beginning of the chapter. What happens when serious upsetting situations occur in the personal life of an analyst? Do these affect the quality of his work? How does he deal with an illness in himself which is upsetting but does not require the suspension of his practice? I recently went through a six-month period in which I had a virus that was debilitating but did not confine me to my home. I dealt with this situation by letting my patients know that I was not up to par. If there was a day I felt especially poorly, I informed them of this, so they could validate their reaction to me and not wonder if it was some transference distortion on their part or some emotional reaction they had induced in me. This is a far cry, is it not, from the nonparticipant analyst? Most of the time, even if I have been in severe physical or emotional stress, I have been able to do my work at about 80 percent efficiency. Especially with experience, a professional is able to transcend his immediate hurts and do a workmanlike if not perfect job. If I ever feel that I am unable to do so, I trust I will have enough integrity to inform my patients of this and to suspend treatment until my personal situation has been settled. I am currently treating two patients whose therapist died while they were in analysis. They strongly resent the fact that their therapist not only did not share with them the seriousness of her illness, but rather went out of her way to deny that anything was amiss.

Other questions raised by analysts deal with two issues that can be combined. One has to do with a recent trend among analysts and other therapists to get their patients to sign a written contract or agree to an oral one that they will stay in treatment for a specified period, usually a month or two. The other question was whether an analyst should allow his patient to explore other therapies in conjunction with analytic treatment—such as body therapies, EST, yoga, meditation, group, couples, or family therapy with another therapist, hypnosis, etc. As I have said, I strongly support the patient's right to do whatever he wishes while he is in analysis with me. Many of my patients have utilized one or more of the above modalities or others concurrent with their analysis with me. They were not always enormous successes, although in some instances they were quite useful and helpful to the patient. As I have said, analysts use another form of double talk about these treatments, talking of "splitting the transference," which means setting up the two therapists against one another, the one all good and the other all bad. If in fact this does occur, it is grist for the mill. In my experience, it has rarely if ever threatened the analytic relationship. I believe that the prohibition of these concurrent treatments or of bibliotherapy, or the need for a contract, are all much more a function of the analyst's insecurity about keeping his patient than they are any of the rationalizations analysts use about them. My feeling is that the patient is an autonomous adult and the analytic process should reward and enhance this situation. He should be free to come and go when and where he pleases. He also should be free to leave me—even if his decision is totally unilateral—at any moment. I believe that any form of contract is a gross and outrageous violation of his personal freedom and autonomy. It very likely was this sort of invasion and encroachment by his parents that made him neurotic in the first place. How can the damage caused by this be reversed by a process whose structure repeats it?

Overall, I seek to supply a patient with an environment unlike the one that caused his emotional difficulties and which is also very difficult to find anywhere but in an analytic situation. I try to respond to him in a way that respects his personal freedom, that respects his rights and choices, that does not punish his autonomy, that provides him with a person who listens to him, communicates with him, cares deeply about his welfare not only because he is a patient but because he is a person, does not exploit him for personal gain, and has goodwill and a sense of humor about his own as well as the patient's foibles. This may seem like a rather tall order but I do not feel it is an impossible one for which to strive. I also feel that the rules of technique of classical analysis, by their very structure, completely prevent it from occurring. The couch prevents intimacy and communication. The rules of abstinence and anonymity prevent a caring egalitarian relationship. The rigid structure punishes autonomy. The financial structure encourages exploitation. One would need an analysis just to correct the iatrogenic damage—that is, the damage caused by the structure set up by the doctor!

15

Conclusion

In the course of this book, I have selected to focus on those contributors to my personal development as an analyst who have had the greatest impact on me. If I were to cite all of the people to whom I am indebted, I could fill an entire page with their names alone. Some I have left out solely for reasons of having to choose very particular favorites, not out of any disparagement of their work.

Certainly a giant in the field who has been largely neglected in American psychoanalysis is Carl Jung, the Swiss analyst. He has a "mystical" orientation in the good sense of the word and was strongly influenced by Eastern religion and philosophy. If there is a candidate for my next love affair among analytic thinkers, I am sure Jung is the prime contender. I have been flirting with his ideas over the past ten years, but have been distracted by more alluring thinkers. I find his ideas about male and female—"animus" and "anima," as he calls them—especially pertinent and appealing. He felt that all of us have strong masculine as well as feminine components and that we are not able to maximize ourselves unless we express both sides. Apparently he anticipated the breaking down of sexual stereotypes by more than fifty years. His theory along these lines is especially pertinent in our time; but it is just a minuscule part of the vast body of his work. I feel that he will be my next hero.

Another important contributor to our body of knowledge was Edith Jacobson, who died recently, in 1982. Though she came out of a classical Freudian background, her work encompasses a great many Kleinian ideas. She has focused on our internal world and how it is populated by representations of ourselves—that is, our subjective view of who we are—and the representations of the people close to us. It is these internal representations that we deal with, not the person themselves or even *our* selves. She clearly has a strong commitment to the subjective nature of our mental activity and the way we deal with people in our internal world.

It would be unwise for me to mention or even list other contributors; I would only feel badly about people whose names I have omitted. Almost everyone who has written extensively has added to our general body of knowledge. My hope for psychoanalysis would be for someone to synthesize the work of all these people into one general comprehensive framework which would include everything and put an end to the internecine warfare among groups that has been so destructive and so divisive in the psychoanalytic movement. Even more, I would wish and hope that psychoanalysis would encourage each practitioner to find his own method, arising out of his own particular personality, to apply this knowledge. Psychoanalysis is an interpersonal treatment, a talking treatment, a means of communication. The impact the analyst has is certainly enhanced by his use of himself in his most idiosyncratic, authentic manner. In all fields people are more creative when they do not adhere to formulas. After thorough training, we should set psychoanalysts free to be themselves in the manner in which they can best impart their knowledge. This will lead to an explosion of creativity in a field that could otherwise stagnate and destroy itself by its rigidity.

Another part of this rigidity is the restriction of the practice of psychoanalysis to the medical profession. There are unfortunately too many medical analysts who are quite adamant about this issue, which is still being argued today in many psychoanalytic associations. I have said jokingly that the only use I make of my medical background is the privilege of parking my car illegally. This is not precisely true, but I rarely have occasion to use my background. Other analysts who come out of psychology or social work or other disciplines, however, are well versed in bodies of knowledge that my medical background did not include, such as knowledge of psychological research and testing, or the impact of social forces on personality. So whatever deficits they may have in medical knowledge, they may well compensate for in other ways. Most of my referrals have been or continue to be to nonmedical analysts. Many of the most prominent contributors to the field have not been physicians. What makes a good analyst is much more a function of his personal sensitivity and integrity, his personal analytic and supervisory experience, than a medical degree. As a matter of fact, the medical model of a healthy doctor taking a superior position to and treating a sick patient is, to my mind, totally counterproductive in an analytic setting. It sets up the dependency and the search for the expert to provide "the" answer which I find inimical to personal growth and self-actualization. That is why I advocate so strongly a more informal, relaxed, egalitarian relationship between patient and analyst. Many of my patients are more intelligent, sensitive, and emotionally intact than I am. The only area of superiority I have over some of them (not even over some of the analysts I treat) is my knowledge and experience in the field. The classical stance very much perpetuates the medical model. The patient is still lying down, as on the examination table, while the doctor is sitting up. The very position is one of inequality. But the analyst's silence, anonymity, and abstinence all enhance this inequality. As I have said before, what is supposed to produce a liberating experience often produces the exact opposite. The patient goes through a long, arduous experience that reinforces his dependency and infantilism. He gradually submits to what clues he picks up from the analyst and becomes a docile child who has sold out on his Self. When the analyst experiences him in exactly the image he would want him to be, he dismisses him as cured. The liberation brought about by dream analysis and the uncovering of unconscious material is superseded by the interpersonal transaction in the room. True, the patient trots out some of his unconscious (the part that is not prohibited by the analyst's counterresistance). He may even experience anger toward the analyst. But this anger is so clearly labeled as transference that we have a psychodrama that is not real, rather than an emotional exploration of the feelings that erupt between two real people. Some of the patient's reactions to the analyst are appropriate reactions to real deficits in the analyst's personality, not simply reenactments of past infantile angers to others. And some others are very appropriate to the bizarre milieu that is forced upon the patient. Many of these problems arise from the medical model. I often say it took me ten years to get over this medical indoctrination.

Why do people become analysts? I suppose for many diverse reasons. My reasons and those of many of the analysts I have treated certainly include—high on the list—an attempt to achieve a cognitive, intellectual mastery over forces which were unleashed in childhood that created tremendous unrest. In many ways, the more pain and turmoil a person has been exposed to, the more open he may be to his patients' difficulties. However, obviously if there are a plethora of anxieties in the analyst that have not been resolved by his analysis and supervision, these can interfere with his effectiveness. But aside from attempts at coping with inner problems, I like to think that people who become analysts also have an *intellectual* interest in understanding themselves and the world in which they live. Practicing analysis is extremely fulfilling in the sense that one is pursuing an area of knowledge that is endless and infinite. Besides this intellectual stimulation, which is constant and unending, there is enormous *emotional* satisfaction not only in helping people find more gratifying lifestyles but in getting very close to very many people in a way that others are not likely to.

If the analyst can be self-revealing and the emotional transaction can be a two-way street, these experiences can be extraordinarily enriching. What other profession can offer so much intimacy with so many people? This intimacy allows an analyst the possibility of giving as well as getting a tremendous amount of affection. Analysis is also a situation that puts a premium on honesty and integrity. I often say that almost nowhere except in my office can I have dealings with people that are direct and not devious or manipulative. Perhaps you have to be crazy to go into the field of psychoanalysis, but you certainly don't have to be crazy to continue in it. The rewards, in my opinion, cannot be matched by any other profession.